Randy Charles Epping

A Beginner's Guide to the World Economy

Randy Charles Epping, an American citizen currently living in Zurich, Switzerland, has worked in international finance for several years, holding management positions in European and American investment banks in Geneva, London, and Zurich. He holds a master's degree in international relations from Yale University, where he concentrated in international finance. In addition, he has received a master's degree from the University of Paris—Sorbonne, and a bachelor's degree from the University of Notre Dame. He is at present the head of IFS Project Management A.G., a Swiss-based international consulting company. He is fluent in five languages: English, French, German, Portuguese, and Spanish.

A BEGINNER'S
GUIDE TO
THE
WORLD
ECONOMY

A BEGINNER'S GUIDE TO THE WORLD ECONOMY

Seventy-one Basic Economic Concepts
That Will Change the Way You See the World

RANDY CHARLES EPPING

VINTAGE BOOKS

A DIVISION OF RANDOM HOUSE, INC.

NEW YORK

A VINTAGE ORIGINAL, JUNE 1992

Copyright © 1992 by Randy Charles Epping

All rights reserved under International and Pan-American Copyright Conventions. Published in the United States by Vintage Books, a division of Random House, Inc., New York, and simultaneously in Canada by Random House of Canada Limited, Toronto.

Maps used on pages xv, xvi, and 73 based on maps in the *New State of the World Atlas*, 4th edition, by Michael Kidron and Ronald Seagal.

Grateful acknowledgment is made to *USA TODAY* for permission to reprint the table appearing on page 46 from "80's Stars—and Dogs." Copyright © 1989 by *USA TODAY*. Reprinted with permission.

Library of Congress Cataloging-in-Publication Data
Epping, Randy Charles.
A beginner's guide to the world economy: seventy-one basic economic concepts that will change the way you see the world / Randy Charles Epping.—1st ed.
p.   cm.
"A Vintage original"—T.p. verso.
Includes index.
ISBN 0-679-73671-9
1. International finance.   2. Finance.   I. Title.
HG3881.E57   1992
337—dc20   91-50215
CIP

Design by ROBERT BULL DESIGN

Manufactured in the United States of America

If economists want to be understood, let them use plainer words . . . [and] address those words less to politicians and more to everybody else. Politicians care about what voters think, especially voters in blocks, and not a shred about what economists think. Talking to politicians about economics is therefore a waste of time. The only way to make governments behave as if they were economically literate is to confront them with electorates that are.

THE ECONOMIST
June 17, 1989

ACKNOWLEDGMENTS

This book is dedicated to my parents, Larry and Jeanette, and to everyone who helped along the way—in particular, to Janos Farago in Geneva and Emmanuele Pignatelli in Zurich (without whose help this book would really not have been possible), and Chuck Painter of Rome, who first inspired me to write it. A special thanks to all those who helped with ideas and suggestions, making this book as "user friendly" as possible: Shawn Engelberg of Portland, Oregon; Garret Tichelaar of New York; Paul Barichman of Athens, Georgia; Del Franz of New York; Otto Bohlman of New Haven, Connecticut; Joanna Hurley of Albuquerque, New Mexico; Elemer Hantos of Nyon, Switzerland; Robert Malley of Los Angeles; Pedro Moreira Salles of São Paulo, Brazil; Jim Ragsdale of Cambridge, Massachusetts; Jean-Marc and Virginia Pilpoul of Paris; Alex Neuman of Zurich; Sebastian Velasco of Madrid; Chris Elliott of Geneva; Rich Rimer of Zurich; Enrique Schmid of San Pedro Sula, Honduras; Benoit Demeuleme-ester of Basel, Switzerland; Persio Arida of São Paulo, Brazil; and Michael Piore at MIT in Cambridge, Massachusetts. I would also like to thank my editors at Vintage Books—Marty Asher, for his vision and confidence in developing and publishing this book, and Edward Kastenmeier, for his gentle and tireless assistance. A final thanks to Tom Header of the Yale Club of New York City for his efforts to provide a safe and comfortable place for me to write *A Beginner's Guide to the World Economy*.

CONTENTS

INTRODUCTION

E VERY DAY we hear more and more about the global economy. Phrases like "economic sanctions," "24-hour global trading," and "international trade wars" appear continually in our newspapers, magazines, and on television.

Whether we realize it or not, the world economy has become an integral factor in our daily lives. From the imported alarm clock that wakes us up in the morning to our retirement funds being invested abroad while we sleep at night, our lives are increasingly influenced by the growing world of international economics and politics. Whoever we are—professionals or homemakers, farmers or college students—we need to understand the basics of the world economy if we are to be effective citizens and consumers.

The first step is to become economically literate. For many of us, however, the study of economics has been an exercise in futility, full of obscure graphs and equations, and hopelessly out of touch with our daily lives. This doesn't have to be the case.

The world economy is really no more complicated than the domestic economy we experience every day. It just seems complicated because it involves different currencies, languages, and political systems. By understanding the basics of the world economy, we can begin to make better political and economic decisions. And with economically literate voters pushing them on, our politicians will finally start making more rational economic decisions, leading to a more prosperous and environmentally sound world in the years to come.

This is not a "get-rich-quick" book. If you want to make a fortune in international finance, you will have to look elsewhere. However, since it is important to understand the basics before undertaking any investment, this could be a great first step to any profitable venture into the global financial marketplace.

This book is meant to be fun and accessible. It was fun to write and it should never stop being fun to read. No graphs and equations will be used, and statistics will always be accompanied by examples to give meaning to the numbers. *A Beginner's Guide to the World Economy,* as the name implies, will cover only the basics. The theories and complicated economic principles will be left to others. Only those concepts found in the daily news will be tackled here.

Although it may be useful to start with the general economic concepts found at the beginning of the book, each section can be read individually. These sections can be read from front to back, from back to front, or at random. After finishing the book, the glossary at the end can be used for quick reference in the future, when unfamiliar terms reappear in the news or come up in daily conversation.

Remember, the world economy can be easily understood. Once we have understood the basics, the world economy can become a great adventure where foreign lands and peoples interact in fascinating ways for all of us. It just needs to be simply explained. Enjoy it!

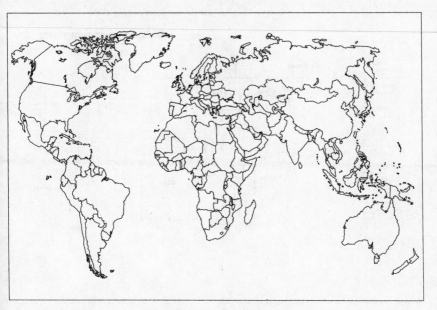

MAP OF THE WORLD

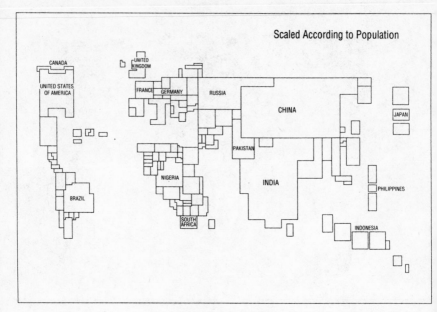

POPULATION

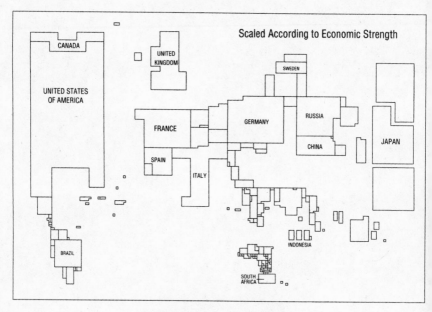

NATIONAL INCOME

A BEGINNER'S GUIDE TO THE WORLD ECONOMY

1. WHAT IS THE WORLD ECONOMY?

I N MANY WAYS, we are all part of the world economy. When we drink our imported coffee in the morning, when we use a foreign-made videocassette recorder, or when we travel abroad on holiday, we are participating in the growing world of international trade and finance.

And it is not only as a consumer of foreign goods and services that we are part of the world economy. The money that our pension funds or university endowments earn from global investments may actually be paying for our retirement or a new building on campus. Foreign investment in local real estate and companies can also provide needed jobs for our friends and families. Even the local athlete who has signed a contract to play abroad is part of the expanding global economy.

The world economy is made up of all those interactions among people, businesses, and governments that cross international borders, even the illegal ones. If we buy drugs—or if we join the fight against drugs by helping Colombian farmers substitute food crops for coca— we become part of the world economy. We also use the world economy to achieve specific political or ecological objectives when we employ economic sanctions to fight racial segregation or the illegal killing of whales.

Basically, whatever crosses an international border—whether goods, services, or transfers of funds—is part of the world economy. Food imports, automobile exports, investments abroad, even the trade in services such as movies or tourism contribute to each country's international economic activity.

2. HOW IS WEALTH DETERMINED

AROUND THE WORLD?

A NATION'S WEALTH can best be determined by looking at its people. But it is difficult to rely on any one statistic. Are the Kuwaitis better off because they earn more money per capita than the Brazilians? Are the French better off if they have more telephones per household than the Japanese? Are Italians better off because they save more money than the Canadians?

There are many different ways to determine wealth. Economists define wealth as what a person owns, such as stocks and real estate, but many people look first to their level of income to see if they are well off. Comparing salaries in different countries, however, is like comparing apples and oranges, because the salaries in each country are paid in different currencies. We need to somehow translate what each person earns into a common unit of measure.

One way of translating salaries is to first compare the value of the currencies of the countries in question. This is usually done by using exchange rates that tell us the value of one currency calculated in terms of another.

Exchange rates, determined by the foreign exchange markets around the world, reflect the markets' view of each country's economic and political situation. By using exchange rates, a salary in yen in Tokyo can be converted into U.S. dollars to make it comparable to a salary in Los Angeles. Or it can be converted into French francs to make it comparable to a salary in Paris.

Because the cost of living varies widely from one country to another, however, it is difficult to translate salaries by simply using currency exchange rates. If a Big Mac or an apartment costs three times as much in Tokyo as in Los Angeles or Paris, a higher salary in Japan does not necessarily mean a Japanese worker is better off than an American or French worker.

It is sometimes more valuable to look at what salaries will actually buy in each country. A salary's "purchasing power" tells us how many goods and services it can actually buy. Comparing the cost of a group of goods and services from country to country, therefore, gives us a more reliable exchange rate, called *purchasing power parity* (*PPP*). The PPP exchange rate is calculated by looking at the cost of groceries and other items such as vacation trips, automobiles, insurance, and rent in different countries.

By choosing this basket of goods and services and calculating their cost in different countries around the world, we can compare the purchasing power or "real" value of salaries from country to country. Although one country may be richer in terms of the amount of money each citizen owns or earns, what counts in the long run is what each person can do with this wealth.

3. WHAT IS MACROECONOMICS?

MACROECONOMICS PROVIDES us with a bird's-eye view of a country's economic landscape. Instead of looking at the behavior of individual businesses and consumers—called *microeconomics*—the goal of macroeconomics is to look at overall economic trends such as employment levels, economic growth, balance of payments, and inflation. The study of the world economy, for example, is essentially a *macroeconomic* survey.

Just as the speed of an engine is regulated by its supply of fuel, macroeconomics is influenced mainly by *monetary policy,* which controls a nation's money supply, and *fiscal policy,* which controls a government's revenue and spending. Control over an economy is essentially in the hands of each country's central banks and government, because they control the money that provides the fuel to keep the economy running.

Monetary policy, the control of a nation's money supply, is managed by each country's central bank. Germany's Bundesbank, Britain's Bank of England, and the Bank of Japan all regulate their money supplies with basically the same goals as the U.S. Federal Reserve: to promote economic growth and keep inflation under control.

Just as a driver uses the accelerator to speed up or slow down a vehicle, central banks control the economy by increasing or decreasing the money supply. By carefully regulating the supply of money to fuel economic growth, a central bank works to keep the economy from overheating or slowing down too quickly.

Monetary policy is essentially a guessing game. There is not one statistic to tell us how fast an economy is growing, and there is nothing that tells us how quickly the economy will respond to changes that may take months or years to implement. Central banks try to keep one eye on inflation, resulting from an overheated economy, and one eye on unemployment, resulting from economic slowdowns.

The economy at large can also be controlled by regulating fiscal policy, government revenue and spending. Although a country's money supply is controlled by central banks, government spending also greatly influences a country's economic growth. Just as a family's economic health is influenced by a parent's earnings and spending habits, a nation's economic health is influenced by governmental fiscal policies, such as taxation, spending, and government borrowing.

For better or for worse, the major economic influences in our daily lives, such as inflation and unemployment, are primarily the result of macroeconomic decisions.

4. WHAT IS INTERNATIONAL TRADE?

WHEN THE Swiss export chocolate to Honduras, they can use the money they earn to import Honduran bananas—or to pay for Kuwaiti oil or a vacation in Hawaii. The basic idea of international trade and investment is simple: each country produces goods or services that can be either consumed at home or exported to other countries.

The main difference between domestic trade and international trade is the use of foreign currencies to pay for the goods and services crossing international borders. Although global trade is often added up in U.S. dollars, the trading itself involves a myriad of currencies. A Japanese videocassette recorder is paid for in French francs in Paris, and French designer sunglasses are paid for in U.S. dollars in Seattle. Brazilian coffee, American films, and German cars are sold around the world in currencies as diverse as Danish kroner and Malaysian ringgits.

Whenever a country imports or exports goods and services, there is a resulting flow of funds: money returns to the exporting nation, and money flows out of the importing nation. Trade and investment is a two-way street, and with a minimum of trade barriers, international trade and investment usually makes everyone better off.

In an interlinked global economy, consumers are given the opportunity to buy the best products at the best prices. By opening up markets, a government allows its citizens to produce and export those things they are best at and to import the rest, choosing from whatever the world has to offer.

Some trade barriers will always exist as long as any two countries have different sets of laws. However, when a country decides to protect its economy by erecting artificial trade barriers, the result is often damaging to everyone, including those people the barriers were meant to protect.

The Great Depression of the 1930s, for example, spread around the world when the United States decided to erect trade barriers to protect local producers. As other countries retaliated, trade plummeted, jobs were lost, and the world entered into a long period of economic decline.

5. WHAT ARE TRADE SURPLUSES AND DEFICITS?

JUST LIKE any business, a country has to keep track of its inflow and outflow of goods, services, and payments. At the end of any given period, each country has to look at its "bottom line" and add up its international trade and investments in one way or another.

The narrowest measure of a country's trade, the *merchandise trade balance*, looks only at "visible" goods such as videocassette recorders, wine, and motorcycles. Trade in visible goods is commonly referred to as the trade balance even though it includes only those tangible goods that can actually be loaded on a ship, airplane, or whatever other means of transport to move goods from one country to another.

The *current account* is a better measure of trade, because it includes a country's exports and imports of services, in addition to its visible trade. It may not be obvious, but many countries make a lot of money exporting "invisibles" such as banking, accounting, and tourism. A tourist abroad, for example, "buys" hotel and restaurant services in the same way as a consumer at home would buy an imported appliance. Movies and banking services have to be paid for just like bags of rice.

The current account tells us which countries have been profitable traders, running a current account surplus with money in the bank at the end of the year, and which countries have been unprofitable traders, having imported more than they've exported, running a current account deficit, or spending more than they've earned.

Trade deficits and surpluses are balanced by payments that make up the difference. A country with a current account surplus, for example, can use the extra money to invest abroad, or it can put it in its cookie jar of foreign currency reserves. A country running a current account deficit has to look abroad for loans or investments, or be forced to dip into its own reserves to pay for its excessive imports. All of these payments and transfers of funds are added up in a country's *capital account*.

The widest measure of a country's trade is called its *balance of payments*. It includes not only payments abroad, but the goods, services, and all transfers of funds that cross international borders. The balance of payments adds up everything in a country's current account and capital account. Since all the trade in goods and services is "balanced" by the international transfers of funds, the balance of payments should add up to zero at the end of the accounting period. Every banana, every automobile, every investment and payment that crosses a country's borders gets included in this final tally of international trade and investment—the balance of payments.

6. HOW CAN FOREIGN OWNERSHIP HELP A COUNTRY'S ECONOMY?

I T IS OFTEN said that the only thing worse than being talked about is *not* being talked about. Countries with open economies could likewise complain that the only thing worse than foreign investment is *no* foreign investment.

When Americans criticize the Japanese for "buying up America," with large parcels of U.S. real estate in Japanese hands, or when the French criticize the Americans for "buying up France," with many

French companies and even Euro Disneyland under American control, they choose to ignore one of the basic components of international trade: the freedom to invest abroad.

Essentially, foreign investment is a result of trade surpluses. When a hardworking country exports more than it imports, it ends up with money to invest in the world markets. This money can be used abroad to buy anything from foreign government bonds to real estate and companies. The United States, for example, has a long history of investing in other countries whenever it runs trade surpluses. However, when the United States began running trade deficits in the 1980s, the billions of dollars spent by Americans on foreign goods, such as video-cassette recorders, returned as foreign investments in the U.S. economy. Despite the criticism these investments received, they did help to keep the American economy running on track and created many new jobs for local workers.

Because there is a natural fear of strategic industries falling into foreign hands, most countries—including the United States—have laws that prohibit foreign ownership of certain high-tech industries and military suppliers. This is usually accomplished without limiting foreign investment in other sectors of the economy.

Countries with trade deficits can often benefit from foreign challenges to make their own industries more competitive on the international markets. Although this is not always easy, reducing trade and investment can be disastrous for consumers and producers alike. If a country restricts foreign investment, jobs and needed capital are often lost to other countries with more open economies.

7. HOW DOES MONEY FACILITATE
INTERNATIONAL TRADE?

C ONTRARY TO popular belief, money does not really make the world go around: the global economy runs on the trade of goods and services. But without money, trade would be a very difficult undertaking indeed.

Imagine trying to send strawberries to France and waiting to be paid with the next shipment of cheese, or having too many strawberries one year and trying to save them to spend at a later date. And how many strawberries is a piece of cheese worth anyway?

These issues can be resolved by using something that represents value. Let's call it money. A mark, a yen, a buck, or a pound—the name is not important. These pieces of metal and paper serve to facilitate trade in three ways: they serve as a medium of exchange; they allow value to be stored from one year to the next; and they serve as a unit of account. The earliest money, shells and beads, served precisely the same role that paper, credit cards, and electronic bank transfers serve today.

Basically, money makes trade more manageable. Strawberries can be sold for money, which can then be used to buy cheese or any other product. By serving as a medium in the exchange, money acts as a go-between for all the transactions of goods and services that make up the world economy.

Money can also be used to store value from a period of plenty to a later period of need. The producer of strawberries who wants to buy cheese at a later date certainly cannot keep the strawberries; they are not going to be worth much when the time comes to trade them. By selling the strawberries for money, however, the producer can sit back and wait. This money can then be put under a mattress or it can be invested to earn interest that allows the nominal value of money to keep pace with inflation—or even outpace it.

Finally, money can be used as a unit of account. It allows for goods and services to be evaluated by using a common measure. Money tells us how many strawberries a piece of cheese is worth. It also tells us how many apples an airline ticket is worth and how many hamburgers it takes to pay for a haircut. Money allows for all goods and services to be expressed in terms of a standardized unit, and worldwide trade is made immeasurably easier.

MAJOR CURRENCIES AROUND THE WORLD

Country	Currency	Value (in units per U.S. dollar)		
		1980	1985	1990
Africa				
Kenya	shilling	7.6	14.7	24.0
Morocco	dirham	4.3	9.6	8.0
Senegal	CFA franc	227.0	378.0	254.4
South Africa	rand	0.7	2.6	3.4
The Americas				
Argentina	peso	1,954	0.8[1]	5,583
Brazil	cruzeiro	65.3	10,400	170.0[2]
Canada	dollar	1.2	1.4	1.2
Mexico	peso	23.1	457.5	2,941
United States	dollar	1.0	1.0	1.0
Asia/Pacific				
Australia	dollar	0.9	1.5	1.3
Hong Kong	dollar	5.1	7.8	7.8
India	rupee	7.9	12.1	17.8
Japan	yen	203.2	201.0	135.6
New Zealand	dollar	1.0	2.0	1.7

1. Three zeros removed in a currency revaluation program.
2. Six zeros removed in currency revaluation programs.

Country	Currency	Value (in units per U.S. dollar)		
		1980	1985	1990
Europe				
Austria	schilling	13.8	17.3	10.5
Belgium	franc	31.6	50.4	31.0
Britain	pound	0.4	0.7	0.5
Denmark	krone	6.0	9.0	5.8
European Community	ECU		1.1	0.7
Finland	markka	3.8	5.4	3.6
France	franc	4.6	7.6	5.1
Germany	mark	2.0	2.5	1.5
Greece	drachma	46.0	148.2	156.3
Italy	lira	929.0	1,683	1,128
Netherlands	guilder	2.1	2.8	1.7
Norway	krone	5.2	7.6	5.9
Portugal	escudo	63.1	158.7	132.3
Spain	peseta	79.2	154.5	95.2
Sweden	krona	4.4	7.6	5.6
Switzerland	franc	1.8	2.1	1.3
Middle East				
Egypt	pound	0.7	1.3	2.9
Iraq	dinar	0.3	0.3	0.3
Iran	rial	70.0	84.2	64.7
Israel	shekel	7.5	1,484	2.1[1]
Saudi Arabia	riyal	3.3	3.6	3.7
Turkey	lira	89.2	579.1	2,874

8. WHAT ARE THE WORLD'S MAJOR CURRENCIES?

THE CURRENCIES of the world's major economies have names and backgrounds that are as diverse as the countries themselves.

The *dollar,* used in many countries including the United States, Canada, and Australia, gets its name from a silver coin minted during the Middle Ages in a small valley, or "Thal," in Bohemia called

Joachimsthal. Just as a sausage from Frankfurt came to be called a frankfurter, the coins from Joachimsthal were called "Joachimsthaler" or simply "Thaler," and came to be called "dollar" in English.

The *pound,* used in Britain, Egypt, and Lebanon among others, refers to the weight used in determining the value of coins, based on precious metals such as gold or sterling. The *penny* has the same origin as the word *pawn,* found in terms such as *pawn shop,* and originally meant "to pledge." A penny, like any currency, is a "pledge" of value.

In Italy and Turkey, the currency is called *lira.* The word is based on the Latin *libra,* meaning "pound," and once again refers to the weight of the original coins.

In Spanish, the word meaning "weight," *peso,* is used to describe the coins that were based on a certain weight of gold or silver. Originally, there were gold coins called *peso de oro* and silver ones called *peso de plata.* In Spain, the currency is called *peseta,* meaning "small peso." The word *peso* is used to describe the currency in many Spanish-speaking countries in Latin America.

In Denmark, Norway, and Sweden, the word for crown—*krone* in Denmark and Norway, *krona* in Sweden—is used to describe the currency that was originally minted by the king and queen, with royal crowns stamped on the earlier coins. Today, the crown has been replaced by other symbols, but the name remains.

The *franc,* used in France, Switzerland, Belgium, and other countries and territories, is based on the early coins used in France that bore the Latin inscription *franconium rex,* meaning "king of the Franks." The coin, as well as the country, took its name from one of the original tribes that settled in the area, the Franks.

The German *mark* and Finnish *markka* derive their names from the small marks that were cut into coins to indicate their precious metal content. The German mark, *deutsche mark* in German, is often called by its shortened name, D-mark.

The *riyal,* in Saudi Arabia and Qatar, and the *rial* in Iran, are based on the Spanish word *real*—which, in turn, was derived from the Latin *regal(is)*—referring to earlier "royal" coins. The *dinar,* used in Iraq and Kuwait among others, derives its name from "denarius," a Roman coin that was worth "ten bronze asses," an item of considerable value in days of old. In India, Pakistan, and other countries of the subcontinent, the currency is called *rupee* (in Indonesia, *rupiah*), based on the Sanskrit word *rupya*, meaning "coined silver."

The ancient Chinese word *yiam* meant "round," or "small round thing." The name of the Japanese currency, the *yen*, and the name of the Chinese currency, the *yuan*, both derived from the old Chinese word, refer to the round shape of the original coins.

9. WHAT ARE FREELY FLOATING CURRENCIES?

APART FROM a few misguided misers like Ebeneezer Scrooge, no one wants a currency "to have and to hold, until death do you part." Currencies are used to buy goods and services, both at home and abroad, and their value is determined in many ways.

It used to be that a currency's value was fixed by its government or was linked to some item of value. This is not necessarily the case today. In the United States, for example, dollars held by foreigners could be converted into gold until 1971. This *gold standard* was meant to guarantee that currencies would always have a fixed value, determined by the amount of gold in each country's vaults.

Most countries had already abandoned the gold standard in the 1930s, when insufficient gold reserves forced governments to adopt a system of fixed exchange rates where each country's government decided on its own what its currency was worth. This artificial system of fixed rates gave way to a free market of currency values when the Smithsonian Agreement of fixed exchange rates collapsed in 1973 and the world's major currencies were allowed to "float" freely on the international markets.

The value of the major world currencies—such as the U.S. dollar, the Swiss franc, and the Japanese yen—is no longer fixed but is allowed to fluctuate freely on the world's foreign exchange markets. Just like a concert ticket on the night of a sold-out performance, a freely floating currency's price goes up when there is increased demand.

Currencies are "scarce" commodities, subject to the laws of supply and demand, as long as governments do not start printing too much money. When everyone wants to buy Japanese stereo systems, for example, the "price" of the yen tends to go up. The yen's value will increase as importers around the world buy yen—with dollars, pounds, or francs—to pay for the latest Japanese stereo systems and video games. Likewise, if Italians should all decide to go on vacation in Florida, the Italian lira will lose value as it is sold on the foreign exchange market to buy dollars that are used to pay for Mickey Mouse T-shirts and Disney World admission tickets.

The free-float system still does not keep governments from trying to influence the value of their currency by buying or selling on the open markets. The present system, sometimes referred to as a "dirty float," is based on periodic central bank intervention to keep currencies from changing value too quickly or from moving out of a predetermined range, such as those periodically fixed in the European Monetary System.

However, like trying to reverse the flow of water, it is very difficult to intervene in the international currency markets. Because of the enormous amount of currencies traded every day on the foreign exchange (forex) markets, interventions by the central banks usually succeed in only slowing down a freely floating currency's inevitable rise or fall.

10. HOW DO EXCHANGE RATES FUNCTION?

I F EVERY COUNTRY in the world used the same currency, world trade would be made much easier. But this is not the case: a Copenhagen beer producer wants to be paid in Danish kroner, and a Hong Kong shirtmaker wants to be paid in Hong Kong dollars.

Currencies, like other commodities such as beer and shirts, have a certain value. The only difference is that each currency's value is stated in terms of other currencies. French francs have a value in U.S. dollars, which have a value in British pounds, which have a value in Japanese yen. These exchange rates change every day and are constantly updated in banks and foreign exchange offices around the world.

The world's foreign exchange markets keep track of the values of all of the major currencies. As some increase in value, others decline. When a French franc goes up in value against the U.S. dollar, the dollar must go down against the French franc. At the same time, the French franc may decline in value against the British pound. Foreign exchange is a constantly changing twenty-four-hour-a-day market with trading going on in hundreds of financial centers around the world, from Singapore to San Francisco and from Oslo to Buenos Aires.

These markets are all linked electronically. Banks and "Bureaus de Change" look at this global interbank market to set their daily rates, which are given to foreign travelers when they change their money abroad.

As anyone traveling abroad will notice, the exchange rate is slightly different if the customer is buying or selling any one particular currency. This spread between the "buy" and "sell" rates ensures that banks and exchange bureaus make a small profit every time one currency is changed into another. By exchanging money back and forth several times, an indecisive traveler would end up with nothing, after losing a few percentage points in spreads and commissions on each transaction.

How do the foreign exchange markets decide how much a currency is worth? Just like other markets, the foreign exchange market is subject to the laws of supply and demand. If enough traders want to buy U.S. dollars, its value will go up, i.e., it will take more of other currencies to buy dollars.

Foreign exchange prices are influenced by economic and political events and sometimes by the speculation of individual traders. Foreign exchange traders, like traders in grain or pork bellies, sometimes "bet" that a currency will increase in value. If interest rates fall in Tokyo, traders may rush to sell yen and buy dollars. If the Swedish economy looks strong, the krona may increase in value. If political turmoil threatens the German economy, the mark may decline in value as investors sell marks to buy what they perceive to be more stable currencies.

During periods of economic turmoil, the world often turns to a particular currency as a refuge. When political or social unrest threatens other currencies around the world, traders and investors sometimes rush to buy hard currencies like the U.S. dollar and Swiss franc, which are expected to preserve their value in times of trouble.

11. WHAT IS GNP?

IN EVERY COUNTRY—from Poland to Peru and from New Zealand to Nigeria—the production of goods and services provides the food, clothing, and shelter that allow its people to survive and prosper.

Some countries produce an abundance of raw materials such as coal and timber while others produce manufactured goods like steel and automobiles. Some countries may concentrate on producing food-stuffs like rice and butter while others produce services—movies, insur-ance, or banking. Whatever is not consumed in the country itself can be sold to other countries as exports.

The size of a country's economy is determined by the total amount of goods and services that country produces. As more and more goods and services are produced, the economy grows—and the best way to measure this growth is to put a monetary value on everything bought or sold. Although money is not the only measure of an economy's size, it is the easiest way to sum up the value of all the apples and oranges, automobiles and computers, football games and college classes that a country produces in the course of a given year.

The monetary value of all these goods and services can then be added up and compared with that of other countries. Since almost every country uses a different currency, the totals from each country have to be translated—by using currency exchange rates—to compare the size of one country's economy to another. For example, the yen value of the Japanese economy can be converted into U.S. dollars to compare it to the American economy.

The measure of economic activity that includes all the goods and services bought or sold in a country over the course of a year is called *gross domestic product* (*GDP*). GDP measures a country's economic activity, just as a speedometer is used to measure the speed of a car. When a country produces more goods and services, its economic activity speeds up. In other words, the GDP increases. A healthy economy grows steadily, over a period of months or years. When growth stops or slows down, the economy is said to be in a "recession."

When the international activities of a country's residents are added to GDP, a wider more global measure of a country's total economic activity is created: *gross national product* or *GNP*. Both measures tell more or less the same story—GDP concentrates on the purely "domestic" production of goods and services covering only the economic activity which takes place within the country's borders, while GNP includes net international trade and investment, which includes everything from exports of movies and compact disks to foreign earn-ings and travel abroad.

GDP and GNP try to measure every legal good and service that an economy produces. A farmer selling fresh vegetables, an automobile dealer selling used cars, a poet selling a new book, a hairdresser, prize fighter, or lifeguard selling his goods and services all contribute to economic activity, as measured by GDP and GNP. At each stage of production, every time that monetary value is added, a country's GDP and GNP is increased.

12. HOW DOES INFLATION AFFECT THE WORLD ECONOMY?

I T USED TO be that signs of a strong economy brought euphoria to the world markets. When factories were producing at full capacity and the number of unemployed people declined, a country would greet the news with joy, confident that with a growing economy everyone would be better off.

But after the severe inflation scares of past decades, when prices rode out of control, governments and central banks realized that an economy that grows too quickly could be a bad thing. With a decline in unemployment, companies are forced to pay higher wages for scarce workers, and prices of goods and services are raised to pay for their increased costs. Inflation is usually highest during times of economic turmoil, such as energy shocks, wars, or debt crises, when there is a shortage of basic goods and services.

Each country keeps track of inflation by looking at the prices of a group or "basket" of consumer goods and services. This is called the *consumer price index (CPI)* in the United States and the *retail price index (RPI)* in Britain. *Inflation* is the percentage rise in the cost of that basket of goods and services over a given period of time. *Deflation,* a decline in these prices, rarely occurs, because companies and employees usually will not allow their prices and salaries to be reduced.

In a booming economy, inflation begins to rise as consumers and businesses compete with each other for goods and services, bidding up prices in their frenzy to buy a limited amount of products. The increase in prices usually leads workers to ask for increasingly higher wages to "keep up with inflation."

The result is often a vicious circle of wage and price increases that end up hurting almost everyone, especially those on fixed incomes, who see their buying power decline when their incomes are not adjusted for the rise in prices. Normally, when governments and central banks see signs of inflation, they try to slow down the economy. They slam on the brakes by increasing interest rates, which makes almost all activities, such as buying new cars or building new factories, more expensive. Higher interest rates tend to discourage business and consumer spending, leading to a reduction in jobs and a slowdown in the economy.

The international markets watch each country's inflation rate very carefully, always looking for signs of stable economic growth and low inflation rates. International investors, such as pension funds and banks, move billions and sometimes trillions of dollars, marks, and yen around the world on any given day, looking for the best return on their investment.

With favorable inflation and interest rates, a country attracts foreign investment and the money comes flooding in. When a country's economy grows too strongly, however, and it looks as if runaway inflation is about to rear up its ugly head, international investors quickly move their money out, preferring to invest their funds in countries with more stable economic growth and predictable inflation rates.

13. HOW ARE THE WORLD'S ECONOMIES
COMPARED?

F A SMALL country like Ireland or Sri Lanka were to win all of
the gold medals at the Summer Olympics, it would mean a lot more
than a victory by a large country like China or the United States.
In the same way, it would be difficult to evaluate the economic achieve-
ments of any country without looking at its size and the resources at
its disposal.

It is rarely useful, for example, to compare the economic statistics
of different countries by using figures in the local currency. What does
it mean to say that during the 1980s the Soviet Union spent more than
forty trillion rubles per year on their military? How does this relate to
spending in other countries where ruble figures mean little?

In order to compare countries around the world, economic statistics have to be related to the country's size or translated into a commonly accepted unit of measure. The Soviet Union's military spending
in the 1980s, for example, can be compared to the military spending
of other countries by relating it to the size of its total economy,
measured either by GDP (gross domestic product) or GNP (gross
national product). It would then become meaningful to say that Soviet
military spending was 20 percent of its GDP, compared to U.S. military spending of 8 percent of its GDP during the same period.

GDP is often used to compare spending figures of different countries because it represents only the domestic production of goods and
services. GDP is useful for comparing countries' sizes because it does
not include the international components of an economy such as
exports and foreign investment, which are included in the wider measure, GNP.

Neither GDP nor GNP, however, completely measures the size

of a country's economy. Illegal activities, such as drug sales or prostitution, are never reported and are consequently not included in these official measures. In addition, work done for no salary, such as housework or volunteer work at hospitals and schools, is not included, since no payment is made for these goods and services. A country with working parents would consequently show a larger GNP, reflecting the added costs of day-care and cleaning services otherwise provided "for free" by a stay-at-home spouse.

Although neither GDP nor GNP is the perfect measure of the size of a country's economy, they still provide the best means we have for comparing the economic activity of different countries, big or small, rich or poor.

14. WHAT IS MONEY SUPPLY?

EVERY ECONOMY in the world is controlled by its supply of money, even one as small as the Monopoly game where players are provided with Monopoly money for buying and selling houses, hotels, and property around the board. The money supply of the Monopoly game, for example, primarily consists of the players' cash on hand and the money they get for passing Go.

A modern economy is based on the use of money. Each country's money supply, therefore, determines how quickly the economy can grow. If the central bank increases the money supply, consumers and businesses have more money to spend on goods and services.

Just as the game of Monopoly can be stimulated by increasing the amount of money available to its players, a country can encourage economic growth by increasing its money supply, which includes currency in circulation and readily available funds such as bank deposits on which checks can be drawn. This "narrow" measure of the money supply is usually called "M1." This easy-to-access money, often called "high-powered" money, tends to fuel most consumer and business consumption and therefore stimulates most economic growth.

Other measures of a country's money supply include funds that are not so readily available, such as time deposits and other long-term investments. These "wider" measures are often referred to as "M3" and "M4" or "L."

Basically, when businesses and individuals have less money at their disposal, economic activity slows down. Central banks usually limit money supply growth in order to slow down the economy and control inflation. In a Monopoly game with less money floating around the board, for example, players will pay less money when buying properties from other players.

On the larger scale of a national economy, less money usually leads to an economic slowdown. When less money is available, interest rates tend to increase—the cost of money increases—and it becomes more expensive to borrow. If it costs businesses and consumers more to borrow money, they will be less inclined to increase spending. In this way, control of the money supply allows a central bank to reduce inflation.

The money supply can also be increased to stimulate economic activity. If the players in a Monopoly game are given more than two hundred dollars for passing Go—five hundred dollars, say—the results are predictable: the "economy" speeds up and players start buying and selling at higher and higher prices. Increasing the money supply usually results in rapid growth and inflated prices.

15. WHAT IS A CENTRAL BANK?

J UST AS a prudent driver keeps an eye on the road and a hand on the wheel, every country's central bank watches economic data carefully and adjusts the money supply in an effort to keep the economy headed in the right direction.

Instead of taking deposits and making loans as normal banks do, a central bank—such as the U.S. Federal Reserve or the Bank of Japan—controls the economy by increasing or decreasing the country's supply of money. Cranking up the printing presses is not the only way for a central bank to increase the economy's supply of money. In fact, in most modern economies printed notes and coins are only a small percentage—often less than 10 percent—of the money supply. Central banks usually print only enough currency to satisfy the everyday needs of businesses and consumers. The U.S. Federal Reserve, for example, has the Bureau of Printing and Engraving print up bills from time to time simply to replace worn-out money in the economy at large.

Since most "money" is actually nothing more than a savings or checking account at a local bank, the most effective way for a central bank to control the economy is to increase or decrease bank lending and bank deposits. When banks have money to lend to their customers, the economy grows. When the banks are forced to cut back lending, the economy slows.

Once a customer deposits money in a local bank, it becomes available for further lending. A hundred dollars deposited at a bank in San Francisco, for example, doesn't lie idle for long. After setting aside a small amount of each deposit as a "reserve," the bank can lend out the remainder, further increasing the money supply—without any new currency being printed. When these loans are redeposited in banks, more money becomes available for new loans, increasing the money supply even more. A bank's supply of money for lending is limited only by its deposits and its *reserve requirements,* which are determined by the central bank.

Central banks often use these reserve requirements to control the money supply. When a bank is required to keep a certain amount of its funds on reserve with the central bank—10 percent of deposits for example—it is unable to lend these funds back to customers. When a central bank decides to increase the money supply, it can reduce this reserve requirement, allowing banks to use more of their funds to lend to businesses and consumers. This increases the money supply quickly because of a multiplier effect: as the new loans enter the economy, deposits increase—and banks have even more money to lend, which generates further deposits providing more money for further loans.

Another way of controlling the money supply is to raise or lower interest rates. When a central bank decides that the economy is growing too slowly—or not growing at all—it can reduce the interest rate it charges on the loans to the country's banks. When banks are allowed to get cheaper money at the central bank, they can make cheaper loans to businesses and consumers, providing an important stimulus to economic growth. Alternatively, if the economy shows signs of growing too quickly, a central bank can increase the interest rate on its loans to banks, putting the brakes on economic growth.

Perhaps the most dramatic way of increasing or decreasing the money supply is through *open market operations,* where a central bank buys or sells large amounts of securities, such as government treasury bonds, in the open market. By buying a large block of bonds, from a bank or a securities house for example, the central bank pumps money into the economy because it uses funds that previously were not part of the money supply. The money used to buy the bonds then becomes available for banks to lend out to consumers and businesses.

In a sense, the central bank creates money every time it dips into its vaults to buy bonds in the open market. Whether it uses a check, pays cash, or simply credits the bank's account at the central bank, the funds for an open market purchase enter the money supply for the first time.

A central bank, unlike other players in the economy, does not have to secure funding from any other source. It can simply print more money or use its virtually unlimited credit with banks in the system. Once a central bank's payment enters the economy, it becomes part of the money supply, providing fuel for businesses and consumers to increase their economic activities. Likewise, when a central bank sells bonds in the open market, the payments from banks and securities houses disappear into the black hole of the central bank's vault, completely removed from the economy at large.

An error in judgment at the central bank has grave consequences for everyone in the economy. If a central bank allows the economy to expand too rapidly by keeping too much money in circulation, it may cause inflation. If it slows down the economy by removing too much money from circulation, an economic recession could result, bringing unemployment and reduced production.

A central bank is much more than a national piggy bank, providing funds for each country's economy. In addition to coordinating the country's monetary policy, it serves as a watchdog to supervise the banking system, in most cases acting independently of its government to provide a stabilizing influence on the country's economy.

The activities and responsibilities of central banks vary widely from country to country. For example, Britain's Bank of England is responsible for printing the money as well as supervising the banking system and coordinating monetary policy. In the United States, the duties of a central bank are divided among different agencies: the U.S. Treasury borrows the government's money through Treasury bond and note issues, while the Federal Reserve Board is put in charge of monetary policy and oversees the printing of money at the Bureau of Printing and Engraving.

The French central bank, the Banque de France, prints and issues the money, but the French treasury makes the decisions regarding monetary policy and bank supervision. In Germany, the central bank, called the Bundesbank, is noted for its active policy of strict monetary control, limiting money supply growth in order to control inflation at all costs.

The Bank of Japan, like many of the world's central banks, acts as banker to the government. This activity is a major source of revenue for the bank since fees are charged for issuing the government's checks and for holding its deposits of foreign currencies. Some central banks, such as the Swiss National Bank, are even partly owned by private shareholders.

During times of financial panic, central banks also act as a lender of last resort, providing funds to shore up failing banks in order to preserve the stability of the financial system. In times of international crisis, central banks sometimes turn to their own central authority, the Bank for International Settlements (BIS), based in Basel, Switzerland. In addition to providing advice and supervision of the international banking community, the BIS can provide temporary funds to shore up failing banking systems. The BIS often provides short-term financing called *bridge loans,* which are paid back as soon as longer-term financing can be arranged.

Central banks also use the Bank for International Settlements to transfer funds to other central banks around the world. The French government, for example, may use the BIS to facilitate a payment to Nigeria, or the Bank of Japan may use the BIS to transfer funds to the U.S. Federal Reserve.

These international payments are handled in the same way as bank payments are credited or debited at a central bank, or as checks are cashed at a neighborhood bank. The system of crediting one account and debiting another makes it possible to settle accounts without having to actually deliver the money directly from one person or one bank to another. In this way, the Bank for International Settlements serves as a central bank to the world's central banks.

16. HOW ARE INTEREST RATES USED

TO CONTROL AN ECONOMY?

I N FREE-MARKET economies, consumers and businesses can do almost anything they want as long as they pay for it. Therefore, by controlling the cost of money—its interest rate—central banks are able to influence economic growth.

In a totalitarian country the government can simply tell its citizens what it wants them to do. But in free-market countries, consumers and businesses are encouraged to increase or reduce their economic activity through a variety of economic incentives. By increasing short-term interest rates, for example, a central bank discourages bank lending, reducing the amount of money available for business expansion and consumer spending. Likewise, by lowering these interest rates, a central bank acts to encourage economic activity.

Banks often borrow money from the central bank to lend to consumers and businesses. When a central bank decides to change its *discount rate*, the interest rate it charges for loans to banks, interest rates across the nation almost always follow suit. The interest rates on loans made between banks—called Fed Funds rates in the United States and interbank rates in Europe—tend to rise whenever banks have to pay more to borrow money themselves.

All interest rates are linked, because money, like most commodities, is interchangeable. Banks and individuals will go wherever interest rates are lowest—basically, wherever money is cheapest—so a change in interest rates announced in Washington will affect interest rates in Singapore.

In the global village of the international money markets, interest rates have become the heartbeat of economic activity, regulating economic growth worldwide. A country's consumers and businesses, therefore, can be directly affected by central bank decisions made on the other side of the world. Foreign investment money can come flooding in at a moment's notice, or be pulled out just as quickly if one country's interest rates are not kept in line with other countries in the world economy.

17. HOW IS FOREIGN TRADE ENCOURAGED?

WHEN EVERY country is allowed to do what it does best—letting the French excel in fashion, the Japanese in electronics, and the Americans in aircraft, for example—the world economy prospers. With free trade, whoever produces the best product at the best price can sell these products around the world, benefiting consumers everywhere.

By encouraging foreign trade, countries expose their own producers to foreign competition, which can be disastrous for many poorly managed companies. This can lead to short-term layoffs and idle factories. In the long run, however, foreign competition usually forces companies to be more efficient and more competitive, helping the country to become a successful and profitable member of the global economy.

Free trade is based on the notion of open markets. With a level playing field, companies in one country can compete openly with companies in other countries to sell their goods in foreign markets.

When a government wants to encourage a new trading partner, it removes restrictions and barriers to its internal market. This courtesy, called most favored nation status in the United States, is provided to countries whose political and economic policies are seen to merit favored status. Countries may also encourage trade by allowing importers and exporters to barter goods. For example, in order to overcome a temporary scarcity of hard currencies in the Soviet Union, Pepsi-Cola traded soft drinks for vodka, which was then sold for dollars, yen, or marks in the West.

When a country wants to encourage its own exports, it can provide incentives to make the products more competitive on the world market. Some countries provide loans or grants to foreign buyers of a country's goods and services through state-supported export-import banks. These "ex-im" banks provide low-cost loans—called *export credits*—that help stimulate exports. These loans are sometimes criticized for going too far, encouraging exports at the expense of producers in other countries.

At times, countries might want to encourage imports of foreign goods and services to decrease international tensions resulting from trade imbalances. When Germany and Japan were criticized for running large trade surpluses in the 1980s, for example, they undertook measures called "external adjustment" to increase their imports. One way to encourage imports is to increase the value of a country's currency, making foreign goods and services less expensive than locally-made products.

Another way to encourage imports is to give the economy a shot in the arm by lowering interest rates, stimulating purchases at home and abroad. This cheaper money usually means more sales of goods such as televisions and automobiles. In countries such as Germany, where many consumer goods are imported, lowering the interest rates can encourage imports of everything from Vietnamese rice to Canadian sporting goods.

Another way to encourage imports would be to reduce cultural barriers that may limit purchases of foreign products. For example, the Japanese government undertook a program in the 1980s to convince Japanese consumers to buy more foreign products (such as U.S. beef) in an effort to ease the threat of retaliatory trade sanctions from its unhappy trading partners.

18. WHAT ARE QUOTAS, TARIFFS, AND SUBSIDIES?

IKE MOST wars, a trade war may bring about desired economic or political changes, but in the long run almost everyone suffers, including those whom trade war was meant to help.

An inefficient car maker, for example, may ask for limits on foreign imports, hoping to keep its prices high without improving the quality of its product. In the end, however, other countries may retaliate with trade restrictions of their own. Consumers and businesses in both countries are then forced to buy poorly made and expensive domestic products. Trade restrictions might protect a few jobs in inefficient industries, but the whole economy often suffers by becoming less competitive on the international markets.

The most common tools for limiting imports of foreign goods and services are quotas, tariffs, and subsidies. When a country imposes a *quota,* it limits the quantity of certain foreign products that can be imported. A *tariff* is a tax placed on goods entering a country, raising the price of imported goods. A government can also use the taxpayers' money to provide a *subsidy* to local producers, making the price of local goods artificially lower than imported goods.

Trade barriers, like walls between feuding neighbors, are usually imposed unilaterally by one country acting on its own to limit the amount of foreign products available to local consumers. These barriers are often designed to temporarily protect local producers from foreign competition and allow them time to improve productivity. The problem is that local producers rarely make the sacrifices to improve their products or lower their prices as long as they are protected from foreign competition by trade barriers.

Although trade restrictions are of dubious economic value, they have been shown to be effective in bringing about political or social change. The refusal of countries to trade and do business with South Africa, for example, was widely seen to be responsible for the decision to dismantle the system of apartheid. Trade blockades can be useful in forcing countries to change policies that violate human rights or international treaties, but only as long as a sufficient number of countries join in the blockade to make it effective.

19. HOW DO BUDGET DEFICITS AFFECT TRADE DEFICITS?

T HE INTERNATIONAL shopping spree of American consumers and businesses during the 1980s was based on a surge in the dollar's value on the international markets. Swedish cars and French mineral water became much cheaper than similar U.S. products, and imports outpaced exports, sometimes to the tune of $100 billion per year, more than the size of most countries' total economy. These severe trade imbalances were caused, in part, by the persistent U.S. budget deficits.

A budget deficit is very different from a trade deficit, but the two end up affecting each other—sometimes disastrously for spendthrift economies. A government's *budget deficit* is the amount by which government expenditures exceed tax revenues, while a *trade deficit* results from a country importing more than it exports.

Most governments pay for their budget deficits by selling government bonds. Although these securities need to be paid back eventually, most governments find that it is political suicide to ask voters to pay higher taxes. They prefer to issue more government bonds to pay their bills. When it comes time to pay the interest on their bonds, governments usually just issue even more bonds, going further into debt. If these borrowings are too large, it can have serious repercussions for the whole economy.

By borrowing to finance its budget deficits, a government pushes up interest rates. These higher interest rates attract foreign money looking for higher returns, increasing the value of the country's currency on the international markets. Imported mineral water then becomes as inexpensive as domestic substitutes. When imports become less expensive and exports harder to sell on the world markets, countries begin to run trade deficits.

The large U.S. trade deficits of the 1980s were part of a vicious circle of budget deficits leading to record trade deficits that gave Japan and many other countries the dollars to spend on U.S. government bonds. In a way, the Japanese ended up trading videocassette recorders for pieces of paper—Treasury bonds that would one day have to be paid back by the U.S. government.

The awkward situation of one country using its trade surplus to pay for another government's budget deficits does not last forever. Foreign investors eventually lose confidence in a country with chronic budget and trade deficits, and when the time comes to pay the piper, the spendthrift country has to begin to pay back its debts. The result can sometimes be a collapsing currency and economic decline. Sooner or later, every country has to decide to limit spending and bring its budget and trade deficits under control.

COMPANIES AROUND THE WORLD

COUNTRIES	TYPE OF COMPANY (IF APPLICABLE)	ABBR.	DEFINITION
United States		Inc.	Incorporated
England, Canada	Public	Plc	Public Limited Company
	Private	Ltd.	Limited
France, Belgium	Public	S.A.	Société Anonyme
	Private	Sarl	Société à responsabilité limitée
Spain, Mexico, etc.	Public	S.A.	Sociedad Anónima
Brazil, Portugal	Private	S.A.	Sociedade Anónima
Japan		Ltd.	Limited
Germany, Switzerland	Public	A.G.	Aktiengesellschaft
	Private	GmbH	Gesellschaft mit beschränkte Haftung
Netherlands	Public	B.V.	Besloten Vennootschap
	Private	N.V.	Naamloze Vennootschap
Italy	Public	SpA	Società per Azioni
	Private	Srl	Società a responsabilità limitata
Denmark		A/S	Aktieselskab

20. WHY ARE COMPANIES REFERRED TO AS LTD., INC., GMBH, OR S.A.?

THE HEART of capitalism is private ownership, and a limited liability company allows people to own almost anything—from skyscrapers to television stations—without risking their personal assets should the company go bankrupt.

An individual, like Henry Ford, might want to begin a small

enterprise and personally retain total responsibility and liability, but once it starts to grow, a partnership or a "company"—such as Ford Motor Company—would need to be formed. The key factor in owning any company is the guarantee called *limited liability:* the owners of a company never have to pay more than they have invested in the company. Their liabilities are limited. When a company goes bankrupt, the owners can never be required to pay its unpaid bills.

The worst that can happen to investors in a limited liability company is losing their initial investment if the company fails. By limiting the downside risk for shareholders, companies are able to attract *equity investors* and raise large amounts of funds called *equity capital* through sales of shares rather than by borrowing money at potentially high interest rates.

The names of companies around the world reflect this guarantee of limited liability. The abbreviations "GmbH" in Germany, "Inc." in the United States, or "Ltd." in most other English-speaking countries indicate that the firm is a limited liability company and investors have nothing more to lose than the money invested in their shares. The "S.A." in French- and Spanish-speaking countries also refers to limited liability by defining shareholders as "anonymous." Since the identity of shareholders can be kept secret, the creditors of a bankrupt company have no right to pursue them for the company's unpaid debts.

Many countries make a clear distinction between public and private companies, with separate designations, such as AG and GmbH in Germany, or Plc and Ltd. in Britain. Generally, "public" companies are those large enough to have their shares traded on stock exchanges, while smaller unquoted companies are said to be "private," even though their shares can be held by the public at large. In some countries, a large company is said to be privately owned if its shares are not available to the general public. In the United States, where little distinction is made between public and private companies, most companies simply bear the title "Incorporated."

21. WHAT IS EQUITY?

OWNERSHIP IN a company, called equity, is certified through pieces of paper—called shares or stock—that state that "the holder of this share owns a part of this company." When the company makes a profit, its owners share in the benefits by receiving a dividend or by selling their shares for more money than they originally paid. When the company loses money, however, the dividends are reduced or eliminated and the share price tends to fall. In the worst case, the company goes bankrupt, owing more than it can pay. The shares then become worthless, and the owners lose all the money invested in them.

A company's shareholders are paid last: after the suppliers, after the banks, and after the bondholders. The risk is that there may be nothing left for stockholders after everyone else has been paid off. The reward is that when a company earns a lot, the stockholders get it all. With equity, there is higher risk but also the opportunity for greater reward.

All investments involve a certain amount of risk, but a stock is generally considered much more risky than a bond, which is an agreement by the company to pay a specific amount of money at a specific time. In contrast to the fixed income of a bond, the return on an equity investment is unknown. To reward investors for this risk, equity tends to provide a higher return, either in the form of dividend payments or by an increase in value, when the company retains its earnings. Stocks often rise and fall in value rapidly, while bonds tend to be more stable. Bondholders are creditors of a company with a guaranteed return on their investment, whereas shareholders are owners, with all the risks and rewards ownership entails.

International equity investment is not limited to the major financial centers of London, New York, and Tokyo. Equity ownership can now mean a share of a fast-food store in Moscow, or it can mean a part of Thailand's booming manufacturing industry. It can be part ownership of a hotel in Rio de Janeiro or a light bulb company in Budapest. Equity means ownership, and ownership is now allowed in almost every country in the world.

22. WHAT IS A BALANCE SHEET?

I F A SIMPLE coconut juice stand on a Samoan island beach were treated as a company, its balance sheet would consist of the following: its assets would be made up of the coconuts and the materials necessary to make and sell juice plus any cash on hand. If anything had been borrowed to set up the operation, these debts would have to be listed as liabilities. Whatever was left over after subtracting the debts from the assets would become the budding young entrepreneur's stockholder's equity.

BALANCE SHEET
GILLIGAN'S COCONUT JUICE LTD.
(SAMOAN ISLAND BRANCH)

ASSETS		LIABILITIES	
Cash:		Debts:	
$10 in coins:	$10	Borrowed Knife:	$10
Inventory:			
10 coconuts	$10		
Fixed assets:			
Knife, Table:	$80	Stockholders' Equity:	$90
	————		————
Total Assets:	$100	Total Liabilities:	$100

All of the assets and liabilities of a company—even one as small as a coconut stand in the South Pacific—can be added up to see what the company owes and what it owns. A *balance sheet* is this summary, a snapshot of a company's position at a given point in time.

A balance sheet is made up of two lists, placed side by side. On the left the company lists everything it owns, such as cash and "fixed assets" called *property, plant, and equipment,* which include everything from buildings and trucks to tools, pencils, and copy machines. This list is labeled *assets.* On the other side, the company lists its *liabilities,* consisting of all claims to the company's assets, from creditors and from the company's owners. The lists end up being exactly equal—whatever assets are not claimed by the company's creditors belong to the owners.

When the company's shareholders sit down to see what they really own, they look at the lists on both sides of the balance sheet. By subtracting a company's liabilities from its assets, shareholders calculate the *stockholders' equity* to see what belongs to them after all of the company's debts have been paid off. This is commonly called *book value.*

When liabilities, such as loans from banks, start to exceed the level of a company's assets, the shareholders may become nervous and sell their shares. They don't want to be around on the day when the company can no longer pay its debts and is forced to declare bankruptcy, reducing the shareholders' equity to nothing.

The purpose of accounting is to provide the company's shareholders with a clear picture of the company's financial health. This "photograph," which is usually published once a year, can be used as a managerial tool, allowing us to see how efficient a company is, and whether it should stay in business.

PROFIT AND LOSS STATEMENT
GILLIGAN'S COCONUT JUICE LTD.
(SAMOAN ISLAND BRANCH)
PERIOD: ONE YEAR

Revenues (from sale of coconut juice):	$50
Cost of Goods Sold (paid to coconut pickers):	$10
Other Expenses (advertising on beach):	$10
Gross Profit:	$30
Taxes (33% rate)	$10
Net Profit:	$20

23. WHAT IS A PROFIT AND LOSS STATEMENT?

ANY ENTERPRISE from a major multinational corporation to a coconut juice stand in the South Pacific needs a summary of everything the company has earned and spent over a given period of time. This overview of a company's day-to-day activities is called an income statement or a *profit and loss statement* (*P&L*).

A company making and selling coconut juice on a South Pacific beach would start its P&L with a summary of all revenues from selling its product. To determine its profit, the company needs to subtract its expenses from its revenues. First, it would subtract the costs incurred in producing the juice, called "cost of goods sold." Expenses such as salaries or maintenance of assets would also have to be accounted for. Other expenses, such as interest on loans, would then have to be deducted.

Finally, *depreciation,* the decline in value of fixed assets, such as machinery and tools, would have to be deducted from earnings. Depreciation causes numerous accounting nightmares because there is no way to determine how much a fixed asset really declines in value over time. Many companies take advantage of this uncertainty to show as much "loss" as possible as soon as possible, reducing earnings in order to pay less tax in the early years of the asset's life. By delaying tax payments, companies can earn valuable interest on their retained earnings.

Once all expenses have been deducted from the revenues, a company can see its total profit or loss. This is the proverbial bottom line. It tells us how much the company's assets and liabilities changed over the course of the year.

Another tool for understanding a company's activity is to look at its *cash flow*. This measures the actual flow of funds—real money—flowing into and out of a company during a given period of time. A company's cash flow, or "cash summary," factors out all of the accounting tricks and looks at what a company really earned. Even though it does not tell us the company's "profit," cash flow sometimes gives a clearer picture of a company's true earnings, because it excludes accounting tools, such as depreciation.

Cash flows and profit and loss statements are essential for understanding the revenues, expenses, and profits of any organization, including nonprofit organizations such as the World Wildlife Fund or the United Nations. Even if profits are not distributed to shareholders, any organization needs a P&L to account for its activities to see whether it is being efficiently and honestly run.

24. HOW IS NET WORTH DETERMINED?

T HE TOTAL monetary value of a company or an individual, anywhere in the world, is referred to as *net worth*. An individual's net worth, for example, is calculated by adding up assets, such as houses, cars, and bank accounts, and subtracting liabilities—mortgages, credit card bills, and other loans.

The net worth of a company is calculated in the same way as for an individual, subtracting its liabilities from its assets. On a balance sheet, a company's net worth is called *shareholders' equity*.

Problems arise when a company's balance sheet includes intangible assets, such as brand names, that cannot be treated in the same way as other assets. Most accountants call these assets *goodwill*, even though the term rarely refers to any good deeds or charitable efforts of the company. The extra price paid by a royal family to acquire one of their former palaces in Hungary, for example, could be called goodwill by accountants. Goodwill also refers to the value of a brand name or a firm's reputation, intangible assets that can be sold just like other assets.

Since goodwill and other nontangible assets are so difficult to value, many analysts prefer to exclude them when determining what a company is really worth. Instead of merely adding up a company's assets and subtracting liabilities, it is sometimes useful to subtract a company's liabilities from its tangible assets: cash, buildings, equipment. In this way, a company's tangible net worth is used to provide a more conservative estimate of a company's value.

Net worth is also called *book value*, because it shows what would be left on the books if the company were to be liquidated, selling off all of its assets, such as buildings, computers, and bonds, and paying off all of its liabilities, such as bills, bank loans, and mortgages. In the mergers and acquisitions game, the wheeler-dealers look at a company's net worth to see what profit can be made from selling off the company's assets.

A company can be worth more than its net worth, however, especially if it has a strong potential for growth, a good worldwide reputation, or a particular expertise in a foreign market.

25. HOW ARE COMPANIES COMPARED INTERNATIONALLY?

T HE PRICE of a company's shares is based on two things: what the company is worth and what it can provide in earnings in the years to come. A company's earnings, like a fruit tree's annual production of apples or oranges, is usually accounted for at the end of each year of activity.

A company's share price is based on its earnings, usually in the form of a ratio, called the *price/earnings (p/e) ratio*. When a company's earnings rise, its share price usually rises, keeping its p/e ratio in line with other companies within its industry. A company with a price/earnings ratio of 10/1, for example, has a share price that is ten times the amount the company earns per year, implying that the stock would pay for itself in ten years' time.

The problem in comparing p/e ratios from country to country is that each country has its own accounting rules: earnings may be understated in one country and overstated in another. It is hard to judge a company's value when the measuring sticks are not the same. Instead of asking, "Is the price too high?", it may be more relevant to ask, "Are the reported earnings too low?"

In Japan, different accounting rules allow many Japanese companies to report fewer earnings than would be accounted for by European or North American standards. For example, many of the Japanese holdings of other companies are not included in their reported earnings. The 5 percent stake that Mitsubishi Trust may hold in Kirin Breweries would be reflected in its price per share, but not in its earnings statement. Japanese price/earnings ratios, therefore, often look high by Western standards.

Another accounting practice that varies from country to country is *depreciation*, the theoretical "loss" companies can report on their taxes as assets such as buildings and machinery wear out. In Japan, companies use an "accelerated depreciation" method to show lower profits in the early years of an asset's life, a practice that is not allowed in most Western countries. If the Japanese were to use Western depreciation methods, their reported earnings would rise considerably. This is why many big institutional investors do their own analysis of financial statements from around the world, recalculating a foreign company's earnings according to a common set of accounting rules. This recalculation often brings foreign p/e ratios in line with those of other companies in the world economy.

26. WHAT IS A LEVERAGED BUYOUT?

A LEVER ALLOWS someone to lift a large weight with a relatively small amount of strength. A *leveraged buyout* (*LBO*) follows the same principle, using a relatively small initial investment to borrow an enormous amount of money to buy a controlling stake in a company.

The key to any LBO is to use other people's money to buy a company and then quickly recover the necessary funds to pay off the loans. This is often accomplished by forcing the management to sell off assets and restructure the firm. The goal is to end up controlling a leaner, more profitable company.

A leveraged buyout takes advantage of the fact that a company is owned by its shareholders, not by its managers. A bank president, for example, does not own the bank, and a factory manager does not own the factory. Anyone who owns enough shares can take over a company. When an investor, or a group of investors, thinks it can run the company better and make more money for the shareholders, it can attempt a takeover. If the company's management opposes the goals of the new controlling shareholders, it becomes a "hostile takeover."

LBO specialists normally buy undervalued companies that hold large amounts of underperforming assets such as cash, real estate, or other holdings. By breaking up the company and selling off valuable assets, in a process called *asset stripping,* the mountain of debt used to acquire the company can be paid off. Many successful LBOs during the 1980s were financed by *junk bonds,* high-yield securities that paid a high rate of interest to investors willing to take a risk on the LBO being successful. If the LBO fails, however, the interest cannot be paid and the bonds literally become junk.

A company's management may try to ward off hostile takeovers by restructuring, selling off assets, and buying back shares to increase the company's share price. These *poison pill* defenses are meant to make the company unattractive or too expensive for a takeover. Sometimes managers decide to get into the LBO game on their own, deciding, "If you can't beat 'em, join 'em." In a *management buyout,* a company's management arranges to take over their own company, borrowing enormous amounts of money to buy a controlling amount of the company's shares.

When a leveraged buyout works, the shareholders are better off, and the company ends up being more efficient and more valuable. If it doesn't work, a company can be destroyed. For example, when it cannot pay its new debts on time, a formerly profitable company acquired through a leveraged buyout can be forced to declare bankruptcy.

$10,000 INVESTED FOR 10 YEARS, BETWEEN 1980 AND 1990, WOULD HAVE PROVIDED THE FOLLOWING RETURN IN U.S. DOLLARS:

INTERNATIONAL INVESTMENT	10-YEAR RETURN	YIELD
Japanese stocks	$ 105,580	955%
Impressionist art	$ 87,140	771%
Various international stocks	$ 54,870	448%
U.S. stocks (S&P 500 index)	$ 47,590	375%
U.S. stocks (growth and income funds)	$ 42,030	320%
Chinese ceramics	$ 41,710	317%
Mixed U.S. stock/bond funds	$ 36,150	261%
Long-term U.S. Treasury bonds	$ 33,200	232%
U.S. money market funds	$ 25,020	150%
Diamonds (rough cut)	$ 17,600	76%
House (U.S. median)	$ 16,530	65%
Inflation (U.S. consumer price index)	**$ 16,410**	**64%**
Gold bullion	$ 7,900	− 21%
Farmland (U.S. Midwest)	$ 7,630	− 23%
Oil (Saudi Arabian light crude)	$ 6,600	− 34%
Silver bullion	$ 1,700	− 83%

27. HOW ARE INTERNATIONAL INVESTMENTS COMPARED?

COMPARING INTERNATIONAL investments, like comparing apples and oranges, can be a daunting task. How can an investment in Japanese stocks be compared to the purchase of silver bullion? Just as an apple or an orange can be priced according to its weight, an international investment can be evaluated according to its total return, the total increase in value plus any dividends or other payments.

College endowment funds, pension fund managers, insurance

companies, banks, and individual investors use yields to compare their growing portfolios of global investments. In this way, all investment instruments—ranging from stocks and commodities to art and real estate—can be compared and evaluated by looking at their *yield:* their percentage increase in value over a given period of time.

In this way, a Japanese equity investment yielding approximately 1,000 percent over a ten-year period can be seen to provide a much higher total return than U.S. money market funds yielding only 150 percent over the same period. To a California pension fund, this yield differential means the difference between meager or generous retirements to its employees. Yield, however, is only one factor to consider in evaluating international investments. The final decision has to take into account the risks and tax considerations as well.

Inflation also has to be considered when comparing international investments. Money is worth only what it will buy in goods and services. If prices rise, money loses its value. For example, in order to have the same purchasing power after a decade of inflation, a $10,000 investment in 1980 would have had to rise to $16,410 by 1990 just to keep up with the rise in prices.

28. WHAT IS A STOCK INDEX?

I T IS NOT necessary for a farmer to examine every plant in the field to see how a crop is growing. It is usually sufficient to look at a few plants to get a good idea of how the crop as a whole is growing. Likewise, an investor does not have to look at every stock traded to see where the market moved on a particular day. It is usually sufficient to look at the prices of a small group of stocks, making up an *index,* which is used to represent the stock market as a whole.

Every major stock market has at least one index that tracks the

STOCK MARKET INDEXES AND AVERAGES
FROM AROUND THE WORLD

Australia, Sydney: All Ordinaries Index

Britain, London: FT-SE 100 (Financial Times-Stock Exchange 100-Share Index)

Canada, Toronto: Composite Index

France, Paris: CAC 40 Index

Germany, Frankfurt: DAX 30-Stock Index (Deutscher Aktien/index)

Hong Kong: Hang Seng Bank Index

Italy, Milan: Banca Commerciale Italiana "Comit" Index

Japan, Tokyo: Nikkei 225-Stock Index; Topix (Tokyo Stock Price Index)

Netherlands, Amsterdam: CBS Total Return General Index

New Zealand, Auckland: Barclays Index

Singapore: Straits Times Index

South Africa, Johannesburg: All Gold Index, Industrial Index

South Korea, Seoul: Korea Composite Exchange Index

Spain, Madrid: General Index

Sweden, Stockholm: Affaersvaerlden General Index

Switzerland, Zurich: Credit Suisse Index

Thailand, Bangkok: Book Club Index

United States, New York: Dow Jones Industrial Average,
    Standard & Poor's 500.

prices of a group of representative stocks. For example, the Dow Jones industrial average tracks the prices of thirty of the most prestigious blue-chip stocks on the New York Stock Exchange (NYSE), America's biggest stock market. Sometimes it is more useful to look at a broader index that takes the average of hundreds of shares. For example, the Standard & Poor's 500 measures the movement of five hundred different stocks on the NYSE.

The prices of the shares in each group are usually indexed, giving more weight to the price change in stocks of larger companies such as IBM or Nippon Telephone & Telegraph. There are exceptions, however, such as the Nikkei–Dow Jones index in Tokyo that simply averages the prices of every stock in the group, regardless of its relative importance to the market. In this sense, it is not truly an index, but actually an average.

In most countries a group of stocks is chosen by a major bank—or a news agency such as Dow Jones in New York—to provide investors with a measure of the market's activities on any particular day. In Japan, for example, the Nikkei index receives its name from the acronym of Japan's leading financial newspaper, the *Nihon Keizai Shimbun.*

In London, the name of the major stock index refers to the leading financial newspaper, *The Financial Times.* In Germany, the FAZ index also takes its name from the leading financial newspaper, the *Frankfurter Algemeine Zeitung.* In most other European countries a local bank, such as Credit Suisse in Zurich or Banca Commerciale Italiana in Milan, keeps track of leading stocks in a stock index that bears its name.

29. HOW DO INVESTORS BUY FOREIGN SHARES?

AS FOREIGN MARKETS have expanded their role in the world economy, many investors are taking advantage of the new opportunities abroad by owning foreign stocks. International investors can buy shares of almost any company in the world, including those in the growing economies of Eastern Europe and the Far East.

One way to invest in foreign companies is simply to buy the shares on the world markets. Toyota shares in Japan or Club Med shares in France, for example, can be bought in Tokyo or Paris by a broker and deposited in anyone's domestic brokerage account. But the foreign share's price is still quoted abroad, and dividends are still paid in a foreign currency.

To avoid the inconvenience of owning shares in foreign currencies, many companies have their shares listed as certificates on local stock exchanges around the world. All of the payments and prices for these certificates are listed in the local currency, just as credit cards used abroad are billed in the cardholder's home currency.

For basically the same price, foreign stock certificates give the holder the rights to a foreign share, called an *underlying share;* when the foreign share changes its value, its stock certificate on the other side of the world also changes its value. For example, North American investors can buy an ADR, an American Depository Receipt, which gives them the rights to foreign shares. In this way, the buyer of an ADR for Toyota does not have to keep track of the yen price of the shares and does not have to read the Japanese newspapers to keep track of dividends. The ADR price is quoted in dollars on North American exchanges, and dividends are credited in dollars to the owner's account directly.

Currency risks also have to be taken into consideration, because the stock certificate's value depends on the currency exchange rate. To return to our previous example, if Toyota stock goes down, a Californian owning a Toyota ADR might still make money if the Japanese yen improves against the dollar sufficiently to offset the decline in stock value.

When foreign ownership of shares is prohibited or difficult, investors may instead want to buy shares in a fund, such as the Korea Fund that was set up in the 1980s to allow foreign investors to benefit from the rise in South Korea's stock market before direct foreign ownership of Korean shares was allowed.

In addition to traditional *registered shares,* some countries such as Switzerland offer international investors the choice of *bearer shares,* which do not require registering the owner's name, or *participation certificates,* which provide dividends like other shares but do not allow the investor to vote at stockholders' meetings and make decisions on running the company.

30. WHAT ARE SOME OF THE RISKS OF INTERNATIONAL INVESTING?

I NTERNATIONAL INVESTING is a risky business. When the Communist economies of Eastern Europe were transformed into free-market economies, for example, their credit risks improved immeasurably, and those who invested first saw the value of some of their investments flourish. In other countries, however, investors were not so lucky as political turmoil and economic chaos pushed many ventures to the brink of bankruptcy.

International investing carries many additional risks along with additional rewards. Global investors, including pension funds and university endowments, need to look very carefully at each country's political and economic situation before lending money or otherwise investing abroad. By removing—or at least identifying—some of the risks involved, the wheel of fortune of the global markets can actually spin in the smart investor's favor. Banks, for example, have made a science of weighing the risks in international investment. When lending money to international borrowers, they not only consider the traditional risks of credit, maturity, interest rates, etc., but they identify additional hazards such as *exchange risk* and *political risk.*

Changes in the value of foreign currencies can provide additional profits, or they could end up eating away the earnings from an otherwise lucrative international investment. A Scottish widows and orphans fund that invests its funds in Tokyo may see the value of its stocks and bonds rise handsomely on the markets in the Far East. But if the yen loses value against the pound in Edinburgh, those foreign earnings may end up being a loss for those who need the money at home.

Exchange risks can also work in an investor's favor. For example, an American investing in Australian stocks stands to gain handsomely if the Australian dollar goes up against the U.S. dollar. The profit from an investment in a strong foreign currency can sometimes exceed the local profit in the investment itself.

Loans to governments and companies in foreign countries also carry an exchange risk if the borrower pays back the loan in a different currency. If exchange rates change, the investor may end up getting more or less in return when the loan is exchanged back into the lender's own currency. For this reason, many loans to Third World countries such as Brazil and Mexico were not made in the local currency. Western and Japanese banks usually preferred to have the loans denominated in dollars, yen, and marks in order to avoid exchange risks.

International investments also present a political risk if a government falls or if new laws are passed restricting international payments. If a democratically elected government is toppled, for example, the local markets may drop like a stone as foreign investment money flees the country.

After all the risks have been analyzed, international investments should provide a return that rewards the investor for the various risks taken. The use of ratings agencies and political analysts helps the investor to calculate risk, but the decision on the return and amount of investment in any one venture must be made on an individual basis.

31. WHAT IS AN EQUITY FUND?

INSTEAD OF putting all their eggs in one basket, international investors often invest in equity funds that spread the risk over a wide range of stocks. Essentially, equity funds allow investors to avoid the risk of losing all their money on one bankrupt company. The funds consist of a whole group of different securities, such as stocks and stock options, that are bought and sold for the fund by professional fund managers.

Many international investors prefer to leave the decisions on foreign equity investment to the highly skilled fund managers who know the individual markets and are better able to avoid costly mistakes. By buying a share in an equity fund, such as a Far East fund or a growth stock fund, investors can diversify the risk over a wide range of companies. If any one company in an equity fund goes bankrupt, each investor suffers minimal loss because of the other healthy companies in the fund.

Politically or socially conscious investors such as college endowment funds may prefer to invest in equity funds that correspond to their economic and political goals. A fund investing only in companies that protect the environment, for example, may be of interest to people who want to accomplish specific social goals with their money.

There are many different equity funds available for the international investor. *Growth stock funds* invest primarily in stocks of companies that retain their earnings and concentrate on rapid growth. In an *income stock fund*, investments are made primarily in already established companies that pay consistent dividends. This type of investment may be of interest to a pension fund, for example, which needs a fixed income for payments to retired people. A *country fund* provides investors with an opportunity to share in the growth of specific foreign markets with limited risk.

There are two types of structures for equity funds. A "closed-end" investment fund (called an "investment trust" in Britain) has a limited number of shares available. A new investor would have to buy shares in the fund through the open markets, where their price is determined by supply and demand. In an "open-end" investment fund (called a "unit trust" in Britain) new shares are simply issued whenever a new investor wants in, and the price is determined by the value of the fund's holdings.

32. HOW DOES BANKRUPTCY VARY AROUND THE WORLD?

THE TERM *bankruptcy* is based on the practice of breaking the bench of traders in medieval Italy who were not able to pay their debts. Once a trader's bench (*banco*) was "ruptured," it was impossible to continue operations. Today, a bankrupt company has the choice of liquidating its assets immediately or it may be allowed to attempt a recovery under a supervised legal framework.

The capitalist system uses the lure of profits as a carrot to attract investors to a new venture, and bankruptcy provides a stick to force companies to be run properly. A company's stockholders share in the glory and the pain of both extremes. When a company makes a profit, the shareholders either receive a dividend or enjoy the rise in value of a company's stocks. When the company loses so much money that it cannot pay its debts, it declares bankruptcy and the shareholders see their investment disappear as creditors, such as suppliers and bondholders, are paid off with whatever funds are available.

In most capitalist countries, bankrupt companies are first encouraged to try to continue operating under legal supervision in order to generate enough money to allow creditors to be paid off. Like having a mechanic fix a broken-down car instead of sending it to the junk heap, a business can often be given new life through a court-appointed restructuring. Rehabilitation, referred to as "Chapter Eleven" in the United States or "administration" in Britain, gives the company the opportunity to reorganize and possibly return to profitability.

Otherwise, a bankrupt company is forced into liquidation, called "Chapter Seven" in the United States or "receivership" in Britain, where assets are sold off—liquidated—to provide enough funds to pay off at least part of a company's debts. The various bankruptcy terms used around the world are:

COUNTRY	REHABILITATION	LIQUIDATION
United States	Chapter Eleven	Chapter Seven
Britain, Canada	Administration	Receivership
France	Règlement à l'amiable	Liquidation
Germany	Vergleich	Konkurs
Italy	Amministrazione	Liquidazione
Japan	Kaishakoseiho	Tosan

33. WHAT ARE CAPITAL MARKETS?

INSTEAD OF borrowing money directly from a bank, governments and other credit-worthy borrowers such as companies and international agencies often use the world's capital markets to borrow money by issuing bonds and other debt instruments. In most cases, this allows them to raise funds at a lower cost than by borrowing directly from the bank.

The international capital markets are used for issuing and trading the world's securities, pieces of paper representing value that could be anything from a bond to a financial future. There is no one specific center for capital market trading, but a series of electronically linked banks and trading floors located in cities all over the world, from Tokyo and Singapore to London and New York, to name just a few. These capital markets serve one purpose: they transfer money from those who have it to those who need it and are willing to pay a price to get it.

These debt instruments can then be bought and sold just like any other commodity on the international markets. The price borrowers pay for money is its interest rate, which is determined by supply and demand. When there is a shortage of money to lend, borrowers have to pay a higher interest rate. When money is plentiful, interest rates decline.

Capital, accumulated wealth, forms the basis for all economic activity in market-oriented, or capitalist, societies. Capital markets, therefore, should not be confused with the machinery and buildings, also called capital, which a company uses to produce goods and services.

The international capital markets bring together borrowers and lenders from around the world. Investors in the world's capital markets can be as large as a British government employee pension fund or as small as a Swiss farmer with a securities account at the local bank. Borrowers, including corporations, institutions, and governments— IBM, the World Bank, or the Kingdom of Sweden—turn to the world capital markets on a daily basis.

When a Swiss investor buys bonds of the African Development Bank or a Japanese pension fund invests in Australian government bonds, money is transferred from one part of the world to another where it can be used for development or growth. In the interlinked global economy, savings need not be kept under a mattress, but can be invested through international capital markets to be used productively throughout the world.

34. WHAT IS A BOND?

U NLIKE A stock, which represents the risk and rewards of
ownership in a company, a bond is simply a loan agreement
that says: "I, the borrower, agree to pay to you, the bondholder,
a certain amount of money at a certain time in the future."

Although almost anyone can issue a bond, large institutions such
as governments and corporations are the most common borrowers in
the international bond markets. Instead of relying on any one bank to
lend them money, they issue bonds to raise large sums of funds, often
in global issues of securities that are sold to banks and other investors
around the world.

A bond is basically an IOU, a piece of paper giving the holder the
right to receive a specific amount of money at a specific time. The
borrower, or issuer, of a bond has two obligations. First, the issuer has
to pay back the original amount borrowed, called the *principal*. Second, the borrower needs to pay interest periodically, to reward those
who buy the bond as an investment. These interest payments are also
called *coupons* in reference to the little pieces of paper attached to
bonds before the electronic markets made such paper transactions
unnecessary.

In order to determine the value of a bond, it is necessary to
calculate the interest paid over the bond's life and compare this with
other interest-bearing investments in the international marketplace.

Bond prices are constantly raised and lowered to reflect the market. Essentially, bonds follow interest rates. A bond paying a relatively
low rate of interest, therefore, will be sold at a discount when higher-
interest bonds are issued. A low-coupon bond, for example, may have
to be sold for 95 percent of its face value, or redemption value, in order
to make it attractive enough to compete with other bonds. In paying
less for a bond, the buyer receives a higher return, or *yield*, on the

amount invested. Like a playground seesaw, when one goes up, the other goes down.

Likewise, when interest rates fall, the prices of existing bonds rise. In a period of declining interest rates, a relatively high-coupon bond would see its price increase, until its yield is the same as other bonds in the market with similar maturity and similar risk. A bond's price may even rise above face value, to 105 percent for example, to make its yield competitive with other bonds in the market.

The interest rate and price of a bond are also determined by its risk—the likelihood of the investment being repaid. The riskier the bond, the higher the interest a potential borrower will have to pay to attract investors. Bonds, especially government bonds, are seen to be a relatively safe investment. In the case of a company running out of money to pay bondholders and stockholders, the bondholders get paid first. A government, in a worst-case scenario, can always pay off bonds printed in the national currency by simply printing more money.

Bond prices are adjusted constantly, allowing them to compete with other investments in the global economy, always reflecting the current political, monetary, and economic environment.

35. HOW ARE BONDS TRADED?

B ONDS ARE traded around the world twenty-four hours a day, usually in trading rooms of banks and securities houses that are connected by an elaborate system of electronic communications equipment. The largest international capital markets are based in London, New York, and Tokyo, but bonds are traded in almost every financial center in the world, from Paris to Bangkok, from Abu Dhabi to Vancouver.

Since it is difficult for bond investors to find individual buyers and sellers, they usually go to professional "market-makers" who buy and sell their bonds for them. Although some bond trading takes place on public trading floors like stock exchanges, most of the world's fixed-income securities, or bonds, are traded by banks and securities houses acting as market-makers on behalf of their clients.

Bond markets are just like any other competitive market in that traders make money by buying for less and selling for more. To buy or sell a bond, an investor goes to a trader who makes a "market" with two prices: a "bid" price and an "offer" price. A trader makes money by buying bonds at the lower bid price and by selling them at the higher offer price. The difference between the two prices is called the *spread*.

Bond traders are forced by the market to keep their prices and spreads competitive. Some markets are so competitive that the bid and offer prices are quoted in fractions of a percent, sometimes given as $\frac{1}{32}$nds.

Bonds are usually traded with prices based on a percentage of their original face value. When the price of a thousand-dollar bond rises by $\frac{16}{32}$, or one half of one percent, its value rises by five dollars. Since the original value of the bond and its interest rates do not change, adjusting the bond's price gives it a new yield. Bond yield calculations are so complex that most traders use calculators to determine which prices bring a bond's interest rate in line with the changing market.

In the international capital markets, some bonds, such as U.S. Treasury bonds, serve as bellwether indicators of the market as a whole. Because of the enormous amount of U.S. Treasury debt issued, international investors prefer to use this market for a large part of their trading and investing. U.S. government securities are said to be the most *liquid* bonds in the world because they can be traded internationally in large quantities at almost any given time.

36. WHAT ARE EUROCURRENCIES AND

EUROBONDS?

D URING THE cold war, the Soviet Union was reluctant to put too much of its U.S. dollar reserves under the control of the authorities in the United States. It turned instead to European banks to keep these dollars abroad, and those reserves became known as *Eurodollars.* Today, any currency held abroad, even outside Europe, is called a *Eurocurrency.* Japanese yen being held in a New York bank, for example, are called Euroyen, and French francs being held in a Hong Kong bank account are called Eurofrancs.

In the 1970s, a huge market developed for Eurocurrencies when Arab oil producers, following the example of the Soviet Union, began keeping a large part of their newly earned petrodollars in Europe. This flood of foreign capital needed to be invested, so banks began issuing U.S. dollar bonds, outside the control and regulations of the United States government. These were called *Eurobonds* because they were issued outside of the country of their currency. Banks and securities houses then began issuing Eurobonds in all of the world's other major currencies such as Japanese yen, German marks, Australian dollars, and French francs.

The Eurobond market grew enormously during the 1980s. Money began to pour into these unregulated foreign markets, settling mainly in London where taxes and restrictions on trading were minimal. Investors also liked the fact that most Eurobonds were bearer bonds. Unlike registered bonds, bearer bonds allow investors to remain anonymous, giving them the opportunity to avoid reporting the interest earnings to the tax authorities at home.

When American corporations found that they could issue bonds more cheaply in the Eurobond market and with fewer restrictions than in the United States, there was a surge of London-based Eurobond activity. Companies and governments from around the world began issuing many of their securities in the Eurobond market, often at less cost than in their home markets.

37. HOW ARE RATINGS USED TO EVALUATE INVESTMENTS?

EXAMINING THE financial documents of companies and governments around the world would be difficult for any investor, no matter how knowledgeable. Therefore, many investors have come to rely on the judgment of ratings agencies that make it their job to evaluate the financial health of borrowers in the world economy.

Anyone lending money, whether to an individual, a company, or a government, needs to know whether the borrower will be able to pay the money back. A bond investor, for example, needs to know whether the interest will be paid on time and whether the principal—the amount of money originally borrowed—will be repaid at all.

Ratings agencies use various systems, usually based on the letters *A* to *D*, to rate the world's companies and borrowers. Two of the world's biggest agencies, Moody's Investors Services and Standard & Poor's (S&P) both provide a "AAA" rating for the most healthy borrowers. Loans to "AAA" borrowers, such as the United States, Switzerland, Japan, or the World Bank, are considered to have the best chance of being paid back with timely interest payments.

When a borrower's financial health declines, the agencies downgrade its rating to keep investors informed of the debt's new risks. Most international funds are invested in bonds with ratings no lower than "A" or "BBB," usually called *investment grade*.

When a failing borrower begins missing interest payments, its ratings will fall to "C" or lower. A rating of "D" indicates bankruptcy. A borrower's ratings can also be upgraded when its financial health improves. As Mexico and Brazil began to recover from the severe debt crises of the 1980s, for example, the ratings on their new and existing debt were increased accordingly.

Since investors are prepared to accept lower interest payments only from the most sound borrowers, ratings are taken very seriously by companies and governments. A high rating usually means a lower cost of borrowing funds. Top-rated borrowers, such as Switzerland or Japan, can issue bonds with lower interest rates than can countries such as Ecuador or India with significantly lower credit ratings.

Essentially, ratings provide investors with a way of evaluating the risk of each investment. A borrower with greater credit risks has to provide increased rewards, usually in the form of higher interest rates.

38. HOW IS GOLD USED AS AN INTERNATIONAL INVESTMENT?

GOLD IS bought and sold around the world in almost every market and currency imaginable: with Egyptian pounds in a Cairo souk, or with dollars on the sophisticated commodity exchanges of Hong Kong or Chicago. Although some gold trading is based on commercial transactions, such as an Amsterdam jeweler buying gold for inventory, most gold is purchased as an investment.

Gold investors range from powerful central banks who use gold to shore up their currencies to individuals who buy gold hoping that it will hold its value in inflationary times. Gold's role has changed over the years. Before banks and securities houses became part of the electronically interconnected global economy, gold served as a "liquid" investment that could be exchanged anywhere in the world at any given time. Now gold is perceived mostly as a "hedge"—providing a stable refuge for investors in highly inflationary times when financial instruments such as stocks or bonds tend to lose their value. When inflation is brought under control, however, gold tends to lose its luster because, unlike most other investments, there is no interest paid on gold. The only possible profit is its rise in value, called *capital gain*.

There are several ways of investing in gold, including buying shares in gold mining companies or gold mutual funds. Most gold investments, however, are "spot" purchases for immediate delivery to a custodian bank that holds precious metals for the investor. Purchases are made on commodity exchanges such as the Comex in New York, or in most international banks such as Credit Suisse in Zurich where trades are executed electronically for clients around the world.

Instead of buying "spot" gold for immediate delivery, however, investors can also make an agreement to buy gold at a future date. These are called *futures contracts* because they are based on periodic delivery dates in the future, usually every three months. Tailor-made futures contracts, with flexible dates to fit the needs of buyers and sellers, are called *forward contracts*.

Spot and futures prices, like a child riding piggyback, tend to move in the same direction, rising and falling with other precious metals in the market. If gold's spot price increases, its future price usually rises by the same amount. In general, the prices of precious metals such as gold, silver, and platinum tend to rise and fall together.

39. WHAT ARE DERIVATIVE INSTRUMENTS?

I T MAY SOUND like a house of cards, but many financial instruments in the global economy are based on nothing more than the value of other financial instruments. Today it would be impossible to responsibly manage any significant international investment without an understanding of financial derivatives like options, financial futures, and interest rate swaps. A *stock option*, which allows an investor to purchase or sell a given stock at a fixed price sometime in the future, is called a derivative because its value is determined by the value of an underlying stock.

A *financial future* is an agreement to buy a financial instrument—such as a stock or bond—sometime in the future at a fixed price. A stock index future, for example, allows investors to benefit from the rise in a stock index by buying, in a sense, all the shares in the index. Just as a gold future goes up in value when gold's price rises, a future on the Standard & Poor's 500 will increase in value when the stock index rises.

The basic idea of a swap is to trade something you have for something you want. A *swap* is a trade agreement between two or more counterparties, usually banks, to exchange different assets or liabilities such as interest payments. Essentially, it allows both parties to obtain the right assets and cash flows for their own particular needs. In the case of banks, this most often means trading two loans with different interest rates or different foreign currencies. For example, a bank lending money to consumers at a fixed interest rate may be borrowing money at floating or periodically changing interest rates. In order to eliminate the risk of having borrowed and lent money at two different interest rates, the bank enters into an interest rate swap agreement with another institution to exchange one flow of interest rates for another.

40. WHAT IS AN OPTION?

I T IS ALWAYS useful to keep our options open—to have the right but not the obligation, for example, to buy or sell something at a guaranteed price in the future. In a time of fluctuating costs, it is always useful to have the option to buy a product at a guaranteed price. This allows us to shop around knowing that we could always exercise our option to buy, if the price is right.

Since we use the option, or "exercise" it, only if it is profitable, it is always good to have as many options as we can. A racehorse owner with an option to buy a new thoroughbred at a certain price could use that option if the horse wins the Kentucky Derby. Or a sheep farmer in New Zealand could profit from having an option to sell wool at a guaranteed price at the end of each season.

In the financial markets, where nothing is free, options cost money. The seller of the option has to be paid for taking the risk that the option will be exercised. On the other hand, the buyer of an option runs the risk of not being able to use it within the time allotted, thereby losing the option's initial purchase price. In general, the option holder's gain is the option seller's loss, and vice versa.

There are many ways to value an option, but it really depends on the likelihood of it being used. An option that no one expects to exercise costs very little. However, an option will be more expensive if there is a good chance it will be used.

Options can be created for anything that has an uncertain future. For example, no one knows if a stock's price will go up or down, so it is worthwhile having an option to buy or sell that stock if its price moves in the right direction. An option's value essentially depends on the movement in value of an underlying asset such as a stock or a commodity.

Two other factors that influence an option's value are *volatility*, the amount of movement of the underlying asset's price, and *time value,* the amount of time for which the option is valid. An option based on an underlying asset with high volatility, such as a stock with drastic swings in price, is worth more than one based on an asset that hardly ever changes in value. Likewise, an option that can be exercised for several years is more valuable than one that can be exercised for only a few months.

Investors need to be careful with options because they are much more volatile than the underlying assets on which they are based. Because an option represents the right to buy or sell a large number of shares of the underlying stock or other asset, its price moves much more quickly—in both directions—than the market in general.

Options originated in early agrarian societies where options in the form of handshake agreements allowed farmers to hedge against the fluctuating prices of commodities such as wheat or grapes. In the expanding global economy, options and international options markets have grown to include an almost limitless number of products including foreign currency options, foreign stock options, and even options on other financial instruments such as stock indexes, futures, and interest rates.

41. WHAT ARE PUTS AND CALLS?

THE INTERNATIONAL markets are being increasingly driven by options trading, and investors in the global marketplace are offered a wide choice of options on everything from Apple Computer stocks to Saudi crude oil and Japanese yen. A coffee company, for example, may buy coffee options to protect itself from unwanted market fluctuations, knowing that in the worst case they stand to lose only whatever they spent to buy the options in the first place.

Call options give the holder the right to buy, or "call in," something—at a certain price and at a certain time in the future. *Put* options give the holder the right to sell, or "put" something into the option seller's hands if it is not worth keeping.

The most popular options on the international markets are those that give the right to buy or sell stocks. Stock call options, for example, give the right to buy a certain amount of shares, called the *underlying* shares, at a certain price during a limited period of time. Naturally, a call option goes up in value when the value of the underlying shares goes up.

Stock put options give the right to sell shares if their price goes down. Put options, therefore, will go up in value when the value of the underlying shares goes down.

Who buys call options? Those who think the price of the underlying asset will go up. If the share prices go high enough, the holder of a call option can exercise the right to buy shares at a price lower than the market price. These shares can then be resold on the market for a profit. Alternatively, the holder of a valuable call option can simply sell the option to someone else, at a profit, and avoid the trouble of exercising it.

Who buys put options? Those who think the price of the underlying asset will go down. If a share price drops low enough, the holder of a put option can buy shares in the market and exercise the right to sell them at a higher price. The holder of a valuable put option can also sell the option to someone else, at a profit, to avoid the trouble of exercising it.

Call and put options give the investor a lot more bang for the buck. Instead of spending a lot of money to buy or sell the underlying assets, option investors can, for a relatively small amount of money invested, profit handsomely if the market moves in the right direction.

42. WHAT IS A CURRENCY OPTION?

ANYONE PLANNING a trip abroad or a business venture in another country would like to know what the foreign currency will be worth when the time comes to change money. Unwelcome currency fluctuations could end up making a dinner in Paris or a BMW import prohibitively expensive.

Currency options allow individual investors, businesses, or merchants to benefit from changes in the value of foreign currencies. By buying or selling currency options, for example, it is possible to fix, in advance, exactly how many Swiss francs or Japanese yen a U.S. dollar can buy at a certain time in the future.

Just like other options, a currency option gives the holder the right, but not the obligation, to buy or sell something at a fixed price, in this case currency. The most common currency options are based on the U.S.-dollar price of Swiss francs, French francs, German marks, British pounds, and Japanese yen.

Like all investments in the international marketplace, currency options can be used for speculation. Investors who believe that a currency will go up in value can buy an option and earn big money if they are right. If a currency goes up in value, the holder of an option to buy that currency, a currency "call" option, would profit. When the German mark rises, for example, its dollar value goes up and the holder of a German mark call option would benefit.

Similarly, if a currency goes down, an option to sell it, a "put" option, would become more valuable. A Swiss franc put option, for example, which gives the holder the right to sell Swiss francs at a fixed price in the future, will be worth a lot if the Swiss franc goes down in value on the international markets.

Currency options can also be used as a hedge to guard against unwelcome changes in foreign currency values. Exporters who earn money from all over the world often need to know what their bottom line will be in their own currency. For example, in order to prevent earnings from being hurt by currency fluctuations, a German automobile exporter can buy currency options, offsetting unwelcome price changes by fixing the mark's exchange rate at a certain time in the future. In this way, currency options allow for the world economy to grow, unencumbered by the many fluctuating currencies used by the world's trading nations.

43. WHAT IS A WARRANT?

I N THE OLD West, a bounty hunter could seize a wanted outlaw by saying, "I have a warrant for your arrest!" A bounty hunter's warrant is similar to financial warrants in that it gives the holder certain rights. While frontier warrants gave the holder the right to arrest someone, most warrants in the world's financial markets give the holder the right to buy a company's shares at a certain price over a limited period of time. These share-purchase warrants are different from normal stock options in that they are usually issued directly by the company, often in conjunction with a bond issue or a leveraged buyout.

Warrants can be attached to a bond, providing a kicker that gives investors an incentive to buy bonds with lower interest rates. Many Japanese companies, for example, have issued bonds with equity warrants attached providing investors with an opportunity to buy the companies' shares. Like other options, warrants are used only when the price of the shares rises past the "striking price"—the price the warrant holder pays for the shares.

Warrants are like coupons in that they can be removed from bonds and sold separately. Bonds that are traded with their warrants still attached are referred to as *cum,* the Latin for "with," and those without their warrants are referred to as *ex,* the Latin for "without."

Another alternative for making bonds more attractive is to allow investors to "convert" the bond into a company's stocks. In contrast to a detachable equity "warrant" giving investors the right to buy stocks with their own funds, a convertible bond gives the right to exchange the bond itself, at a fixed price and at a fixed time, into a certain amount of the company's shares. The purpose of warrants and convertible bonds is to offer investors a future reward—usually in the form of the company's shares—for accepting a lower interest on the company's bonds. Obviously, a country or international organization which does not have any shares would never be able to issue warrants or convertible bonds.

In the international markets, warrants are bought and sold in many different currencies, most notably Swiss francs, U.S. dollars, and Japanese yen. Many of the warrants traded on the New York Stock Exchange, for example, were issued in U.S. dollars by American companies looking for funds to finance mergers and acquisitions. Investors who buy these equity warrants are given the right to buy the merged company's shares at a point in the future, assuming they become more profitable.

The real value of a warrant is its time factor. When a company issues a warrant to buy its shares, it is providing a window of opportunity for investors to wait for the share prices to rise. The more time the investor has to exercise a warrant, the more valuable it is.

44. WHO INVESTS IN THE GLOBAL

MARKETPLACE?

WHEN ALL is said and done, there are only three reasons for investing in the international marketplace: speculation, hedging, and arbitrage.

Most investors in the international marketplace are speculators. They believe the market is heading in a certain direction, and they buy or sell in that belief. A Dutch pension fund buys shares on the New York Stock Exchange, for example, hoping to profit from an expected rise in the U.S. market. However, there is no way of knowing what will actually happen, and speculators never all agree on one particular direction or degree of movement in the international markets. Speculators take a risk. If the market moves in the right direction, they make a profit. If not, they lose.

The frenzied activity of speculators is balanced by other players in the international markets, hedgers and arbitragers, who seek to avoid risks.

In contrast to speculators, hedgers have no idea where prices will go, but want to protect themselves from a move in the wrong direction. For an elderly Canadian retiree, a logical hedge against inflation would be owning a house that would go up in value as the value of a fixed-income pension declined. Exporters may also want to hedge future foreign currency earnings by buying currency options. The role of a hedge is to remove risk by making investments that balance the potential losses of other investments.

Arbitragers, on the other hand, try to take advantage of discrepancies in the market while avoiding risk. They buy in one market where something is cheap and sell it in another where the price is more expensive. A German tourist, for example, may be able to take advantage of price and currency differences by buying German-made compact disks in New York and selling them back to friends at home. Arbitragers take no risks because they buy and sell at the same time, taking advantage of market inefficiencies around the world. The term *arbitrager* is also used to describe takeover specialists who buy and sell undervalued companies.

Markets are usually made more efficient by the activities of speculators, hedgers, and arbitragers. For example, if the markets consisted only of hedgers, prices could rise and fall out of control. Speculators keep the market from becoming a one-way street by buying or selling whenever prices look attractive. And arbitragers keep all the world's markets in line with each other by buying in one where the prices are too low and selling in another where prices have become too high.

45. WHAT ARE THE FORCES BEHIND EUROPEAN ECONOMIC UNITY?

UNITING A continent with more than thirty-five countries and almost as many languages, currencies, cultures, and political systems is not an easy task. Apart from brief periods of pan-European military rule—such as the Roman or the Napoleonic empires—Europe has been divided by sturdy political and ethnic barriers that defied every attempt at unification. England, for example, has often preferred to maintain closer relations with its former colonies around the world than with its European neighbors. Other countries such as Switzerland have sought to preserve their independence and neutrality at all costs.

By the end of the 1980s, however, the continent of Europe found itself completely transformed by the political and economic upheaval in the formerly Communist countries of Eastern Europe and by the decision to create a barrier-free market in the Common Market countries of Western Europe.

MAP OF EUROPE

This rapid pace of change in Europe was, in part, brought on by outside economic forces. During the 1980s, Western Europe looked abroad and saw the United States creating millions of jobs and expanding rapidly in the Pacific Rim. In the Far East, Japan was booming and had become the second largest economy in the free world. The fear of being left behind sparked a renewed drive toward European economic integration.

At the same time, economic failure pushed the Eastern European members of the Soviet bloc—the U.S.S.R., Poland, Hungary, East Germany, Bulgaria, Romania, and Czechoslovakia—toward a major economic restructuring, called *perestroika* by Soviet president Mikhail

Gorbachev. The free-market economic systems introduced throughout Eastern Europe at the end of the 1980s brought with them sweeping political and social changes.

The quest for European unity has involved three distinct groups of countries: the members of the European Community (EC), the Western European countries that had not joined the EC, and the formerly Communist countries of Eastern Europe. Uniting these nations would produce the most powerful economic bloc in the world. With a total population and economy exceeding that of Japan or the United States, an integrated Europe would be an economic superpower.

46. WHAT IS THE EUROPEAN COMMUNITY?

FRENCH PRESIDENT Charles de Gaulle used to complain that it was impossible to govern a country that produced 385 different cheeses. Imagine, then, joining France to several other European countries to form a common market of many different languages, cultures, bureaucracies, and legal systems. The European Community (EC) has succeeded, however, in joining together a group of Western European countries in an economic and political union that has come close to achieving the age-old dream of a "United States" of Europe.

The EC had its beginning in 1957 when six countries—Belgium, France, the Netherlands, Italy, Luxembourg, and West Germany— signed the Treaty of Rome to form the European Coal and Steel Community, later called the European Economic Community (EEC). Originally, the EEC was intended to be a customs union, removing tariffs and quotas on trade among its member countries.

As the EEC grew during the 1970s and 1980s to include Britain, Ireland, Denmark, Greece, Spain, and Portugal, it became known as the European Community or EC. The original treaties were expanded

by a variety of political, agricultural, industrial, and monetary agreements, including the Common Agricultural Policy (CAP) that guaranteed large subsidies to European farmers.

In order to simplify the bookkeeping, the European Currency
Unit (ECU) was created, with an official value based on a "basket" of
currencies so that it would be more stable than any one currency.
Subsequently, it became a popular currency in its own right, with
"ecu" bonds, bank accounts, and checking accounts.

Eventually, the member states of the European Community decided to consolidate into an economic and political union, similar to
the United States or Canada. They decided that the best way to
encourage trade and economic growth was to remove all barriers,
economic or otherwise, between member countries. The plan to remove all barriers to movements of goods, people, services, and money
within the community, known popularly as "Europe 1992," came to
symbolize this drive for a revitalized Europe.

By removing all internal barriers, the EC would create a truly
common market that would enjoy all the advantages of standard regulations, industries, financial systems, transportation, communications,
and taxes. In finally accepting integration, the countries of the European Community agreed to surrender a part of their national sovereignty in order to achieve something they perceived to be of far greater
value: economic and political strength.

Although the official purpose of the common market was to remove trade barriers, it was feared that the EC would build a protec-
tionist wall of laws to keep out foreign trade and competition. The fear
of this "fortress Europe" led many trading partners to form trading
blocs of their own. While the United States looked to Canada and
Latin America to form its own barrier-free market, Japan moved to
strengthen its trading ties with other countries in Asia.

Those European countries that had avoided EC membership also
feared being left out in the cold. The richest non-EC countries—
Austria, Finland, Iceland, Liechtenstein, Norway, Sweden, and Switzerland—had their own free-trade club. The goal of this group, called
the European Free Trade Association (EFTA), was to promote trade

by removing tariffs and quotas without taking away political and military independence.

Although their advanced industrial economies and free democratic political systems would have made them logical members of the European Community, many members of the EFTA were afraid of losing their cherished political independence. Some countries, such as Switzerland, saw EC membership as a serious threat to their official neutrality.

At first, some EFTA countries decided to apply on their own for full membership in the European Community. Others decided to try to develop special trade agreements that would allow them to have access to the EC market while still retaining their neutrality and independence. Eventually, the EFTA and the EC signed an agreement to form an expanded common market, the European Economic Area (EEA), that would remove almost all internal barriers to the member countries, comprising virtually all of Western Europe.

The Eastern European countries, finding the doors for full EC membership locked, requested special trade conditions for entry into the lucrative market in the West. The EC actively promoted this idea of economic enfranchisement, which would allow the other countries in Europe to trade with the EC without granting them full membership. In this way, instead of being left out in the cold, the non-EC countries could keep doing business with the European Community without overloading it with too many new members.

47. HOW DO COMMUNIST ECONOMIES MAKE THE TRANSITION TO CAPITALISM?

WHEN THE former Soviet Union and the countries of Eastern Europe retreated from communism at the end of the 1980s, their worst-case scenario began with economics, not politics. One of their worst fears was that the difficult economic transition from communism to capitalism would jeopardize their newly won political freedom, a fear borne out by the failed old-guard coup in the Soviet Union in 1991.

The transition from communism to capitalism involves more than just changing a form of government: a country's whole political, social, and economic structure has to be transformed. Although it has been used for a wide variety of political purposes, communism is basically an economic system that was meant to provide an alternative to the exploitations of unbridled capitalism. Instead of letting the markets make the major economic decisions, a communist economy puts decision-making power in the hands of the central government in the hopes of creating a more egalitarian "communal" society.

The Communist system was based on an economic and social theory, developed by Karl Marx in the nineteenth century, that called for a takeover of the state by the workers. This "dictatorship of the proletariat" would then pave the way to utopian socialism. The goal was to replace the pain and inequalities of capitalism with "communism," a decentralized community-based system where economic life is organized on this principle: "from each according to his abilities, to each according to his needs."

Although Communist central planning did bring about strong economic growth in some countries—such as in the rapidly industrializing Soviet Union of the 1920s and 1930s—it often resulted in long-term inefficiency and economic stagnation. The central planners concentrated on building industrial dinosaurs, such as steel plants, automobile factories, or shipyards, that employed millions of workers but generally produced inferior quality products and rampant pollution. The Communist countries of Eastern Europe saw their modest postwar growth outstripped by the dazzling wealth and power of their capitalist neighbors to the West.

The failure to "deliver the goods" led to the fall of most Communist governments by the end of the 1980s. But the eagerly awaited prosperity of the free-market systems that replaced them was a long time coming. In their drive to privatize state industries and remove restrictions on ownership and investments, many Eastern European countries experienced painful economic recession. Their transition from communism to capitalism was often hindered by a crumbling infrastructure, rising unemployment, hyperinflation, and internal dissension. Since most employees had lived all of their lives under totalitarianism, they were unable to understand even the basics of capitalism and democracy and were reluctant to give up guaranteed jobs and social welfare for the promise of capitalist economic growth.

Some countries opted for a hybrid economic system. During an interim period, the government would provide an economic safety net while moving forward slowly to reform the economy. This combination of socialism and capitalism was inspired by the successful economic system of Scandinavian countries such as Sweden, which has been able to combine the advantages of socialism with the dynamism of the free market.

Other countries opted to go all the way and make an immediate transition to capitalism. The goal was to quickly transform the economy—and its society—before reactionary members of the former ruling elites had a chance to attempt to force a return to authoritarian rule, through a popular uprising or a coup d'état, for example. Although they risked popular discontent and many years of economic austerity, most countries found that the only way to overcome the decades of economic mismanagement was a complete transition to a free-market economy—with free prices, currency convertability, and privatization—where the people and the markets are allowed to make all of the decisions, no matter how painful.

48. WHAT IS THE PACIFIC RIM ECONOMY?

OVER THE past three thousand years, the world has changed its main center of activity many times. The world economy was once centered around the Mediterranean, where Egypt, Greece, and Rome based their prosperous economies on seafaring trade. At other times, international trade and commerce made parts of China, India, and the Middle East centers of vast wealth and power.

With European expansion into the New World, following Columbus's voyage of 1492—and with the rise of the great trading nations of England, Holland, Spain, and Portugal—the Atlantic became the center for international trade and commerce. This continued throughout the Industrial Revolution as the United States and its major trading partners in northern Europe built the world's most advanced and wealthiest nations on the Atlantic's edge.

With the dramatic rise of Japan and the other Asian and Pacific economies after World War II, the Americas began to turn their attention to the Pacific for their primary economic activity. The United States, Canada, Mexico, Chile, Australia, New Zealand, South Korea, Hong Kong, Thailand, Taiwan, Singapore, China, and Japan became major trading nations, all located on the Pacific Rim. By the end of the 1980s the trade between these economies constituted almost half of the world's total trade and the Pacific Rim countries produced a large part of the world's output of goods and services.

The rapid economic growth of such Pacific Rim countries as Japan, Hong Kong, South Korea, and Taiwan was based essentially on exports. By efficiently producing large amounts of consumer goods, these countries succeeded in building up enormous trade surpluses. South Korea, for example, decided to concentrate its economic production on consumer goods such as televisions and VCRs that could be sold to affluent consumers in Europe and North America.

The success of this export-led economic growth was based on a hardworking, low-wage work force, combined with rapid technological advances and improved access to world trade. As these rapidly industrializing economies became more advanced, subsequent growth began to rely more on internal markets and a service-based economy, much like their wealthy neighbors across the Pacific in Australia, New Zealand, and North America.

The elite club of Pacific Rim powerhouses has gradually expanded to include groups such as Asia's "Four Tigers": South Korea, Singapore, Taiwan, and Hong Kong. Once backward, low-income countries, the "Four Tigers" made such rapid economic progress in the 1980s that they were put in the select group of Third World countries called Newly Industrialized Countries (NICs).

Another group of rapidly growing Southeast Asian countries is called ASEAN, or Association of South East Asian Nations. This economic and political alliance, consisting of Brunei, Indonesia, Malaysia, the Philippines, Singapore, and Thailand, was set up to encourage trade and economic growth among its members. The economic growth rates of several ASEAN countries, Thailand and Malaysia in particular, have been among the highest in the world.

Realizing that their economies have a long way to go to catch up with industrial giants like Japan and the United States, the rapidly growing countries of the Pacific Rim have made many efforts to remove trade barriers. Just as the countries of Western Europe formed the Common Market to stimulate economic growth, the Newly Industrialized Countries of the Pacific Rim have turned to regional trade alliances in order to share in the political and economic advantages of expanded international trade.

49. WHAT IS JAPAN INC.?

THE EXTRAORDINARY success of Japan's postwar economy can be traced—in part—to the alliance of its government and private sector in a giant enterprise, often referred to as "Japan Inc." Japan's economic strength is based on its mercantilist policy of encouraging exports while avoiding imports of goods and services from abroad. Like any new kid on the block, Japan has angered many trading partners by the overwhelming size of these trade surpluses.

The success of the Japanese export machine results largely from a strictly controlled national effort led by the Japanese Ministry for International Trade and Industry (MITI). Some competitors say that the Japanese export machine has worked too well, taking advantage of the world system of free trade while keeping a complex set of trade barriers to imports at home. The Japanese say that the rest of the world buys Japanese products simply because they are better-made and are sold at competitive prices on the world's markets, using the age-old argument, "Build a better mousetrap, and the world will beat a path to your door."

The high quality of many Japanese products can be partly explained by the long-term view that most Japanese companies take in developing and manufacturing new products. Many American companies, such as those in the automobile industry, have been criticized for looking for short-term profits and failing to pursue the long-term research and development needed to bring competitive products to the world markets.

Foreign products marketed in Japan may also encounter hidden cultural barriers. For example, many Japanese consumers are wary of foreign products and their perceived inferior quality. There are also many layers of protectionism stemming from the Japanese practice of cross-ownership of much of its industry, called *keiretsu,* where a company will buy products from other companies in its group, rather than importing cheaper goods from abroad.

In the long run, however, most trade surpluses—including Japan's—can be traced to efficiency and hard work. As long as countries have different laws, certain barriers will always exist. Instead of putting up trade barriers or "bashing" countries in the world economy, it is usually more productive to cooperate with all of the players to create a truly level playing field open to every country in the world.

50. WHAT IS THE NORTH AMERICAN
FREE TRADE AREA?

THE ADVANTAGES of free trade are seldom more apparent than in countries with vastly different climates and economic infrastructures. In North America, stretching from the cold arctic tundra to balmy Caribbean shores, a free trade area would be essential if countries are to take advantage of each other's strengths. Instead of wasting precious labor and resources trying to grow bananas or tobacco in the cold Yukon, for example, Canadians are much better off importing these goods from their warmer neighbors to the south.

It may not be as clear but it is no less true that imports of manufactured appliances from Mexico or automobiles from the United States also make the Canadian economy better off. This logic holds, however, only if Canadians have the freedom to export goods and services to the United States and Mexico. By exporting products at which they hold a competitive advantage, such as timber, banking services, sporting goods, and maple syrup, Canadians earn precious foreign exchange—allowing them to import bananas and manufactured goods from Mexico and tobacco and automobiles from the United States.

By signing a landmark agreement in 1988, the United States and Canada agreed to the complete removal of barriers to trade. When the Mexican government saw the political and economic benefits of such an association with its neighbors to the north, plans were made to create a North American Free Trade Area (NAFTA) stretching from the Yukon to the Yucatán.

Although much North American trade was already tariff free, the pact was seen to reinforce free-market reforms and to further stimulate cross-border economic activity. Instead of taking jobs away from workers in the United States and Canada, for example, it was shown that a growing Mexican economy would provide more jobs for its people at home, reducing immigration northward. By the late 1980s, many companies in Dallas, Houston, and Austin, Texas, saw their exports rise sharply as the Mexican economy grew, creating jobs on both sides of the border.

The long-term goal in setting up NAFTA was to remove barriers to trade worldwide. Unlike the European Community's structure, which put up common trade barriers to countries outside their economic "fortress," NAFTA would concentrate only on removing internal barriers and not to adopt a common market strategy with standardized laws and free movement of people from one country to another.

Inspired by the success of their free-trade neighbors to the north, other countries in the Western Hemisphere subsequently moved to create or revive free-trade associations, including: Mercosur in South America's southern cone, the Andean Pact, the Central American Common Market, and the Caribbean Community (CARICOM). Eventually, a barrier-free market could be established in the Western Hemisphere, stretching from Antarctica to the North Pole.

51. WHAT IS THE THIRD WORLD?

THE TERM *Third World* was based on the idea that the "first" and "second" worlds were made up of the free-market and centrally planned countries with advanced industrial economies. This developed world was seen to include most of the countries of Eastern and Western Europe as well as Australia, New Zealand, Japan, the United States, and Canada.

The developing and relatively poor countries that are said to make up the Third World can be divided into three groups: those developing rapidly, those developing moderately, and the poorest few whose economies are not developing at all.

At the top of the list of Third World nations are the rapidly developing countries called Newly Industrialized Countries (NIC). Most lists of NICs include Brazil, Argentina, Hong Kong, Israel, Singapore, South Africa, South Korea, Taiwan, Thailand, and Yugoslavia. These "lucky few" are seen to be on their way to joining the ranks of the advanced economies of the world.

The bulk of the Third World consists of a large group of moderately developing economies that includes most of the countries in Africa, Asia, and Latin America. The most populous countries in this group are India, China, Indonesia, and Malaysia, which together comprise more than half of the world's population.

At the bottom of the list are the world's poorest countries, found mainly in sub-Saharan Africa, which have so few resources and so little money that it is virtually impossible for them to develop at all. In Somalia and Sudan, for example, there are essentially no natural resources on which to base economic growth. This group is sometimes called the "Fourth World."

Although the Third World comprises three quarters of the world's population and 90 percent of the world's population growth, it provides only 20 percent of the world's economic production. And even though the Third World holds much of the world's natural resources—including vast petroleum reserves in Latin America, Asia, and the Middle East—many raw materials from the Third World are shipped abroad for consumption in the world's wealthier and more developed countries.

52. WHAT ARE THE ROOTS OF THIRD WORLD

POVERTY?

ECONOMIC AND political misjudgment can be blamed for much of the Third World's poverty, but an important factor has also been the population explosion, which caused many developing countries to see their populations double in as little as twenty years. This growth was due mainly to lack of birth control, improved medical care, and declining mortality rates.

Extreme poverty in the Third World has led many parents to create ever larger families, hoping that their children could work and increase family income. But the economic opportunities were often not available, and unemployed children and their parents ended up moving into already overcrowded Third World cities in a fruitless search for work.

By the end of the 1980s, most Third World nations found themselves in a vicious circle of poverty and overpopulation, with no hope in sight. The flood of poor families into major Third World cities put additional strains on the economic infrastructure. Growing urban areas like Bombay, São Paulo, and Shanghai became centers of glaring poverty and unemployment with extensive slums and squatter settlements ringing overgrown and polluted city centers.

Saddled with enormous debt payments, hyperinflation, surging populations, and mounting unemployment, many Third World countries in the late 1980s struggled just to keep their economies afloat. In many cases, with no money available for investment, even the infrastructure, such as roads and water systems, literally began to fall apart. The solution for many overburdened Third World governments was to simply increase debt in order to keep money flowing. But rampant inflation often ends up eroding most of these efforts, creating an ever-widening gap between the Third World's poorest and richest nations.

While many economies in Latin America, Africa, and Asia stagnated, the economies of the elite developing countries of the Pacific Rim rose to levels that rivaled Japan's in the 1960s. The success of many Third World countries in growing their way out of poverty can be traced largely to effective economic policy. By efficiently producing and exporting manufactured goods, countries such as Taiwan and Korea earned enormous amounts of money that they have been able to reinvest in their growing economies.

53. WHERE DID THE THIRD WORLD DEBT COME FROM?

DURING THE oil booms of the 1970s, the oil-rich Arab countries of the Middle East turned to the world's major banks, primarily in the United States and Europe, to provide a safe home for their newly earned petrodollars.

These interest-bearing deposits, sitting in the coffers of Western banks, needed to be recycled—lent to interest-paying borrowers—in order to earn money for the banks. Many banks with large deposits of petrodollars chose to make enormous loans to the developing countries of the Third World, loans that were used, in part, to pay for those countries' ever-increasing oil imports.

At the time, loans with floating interest rates looked irresistible to the developing countries: interest rates were so low, they were not even keeping up with inflation. Borrowing money looked like a no-lose situation. Latin American countries with strong growth rates such as Mexico and Brazil were able to borrow tens of billions of dollars at bargain-basement prices.

The goal of the debtor governments was to borrow as much as possible in a gamble: by borrowing cheap money, they hoped to build a new infrastructure and new industries that would produce enough exports to pay back the loans in the future.

Brazil, for example, during the 1960s and 1970s, had one of the highest growth rates in the world. Its economy was producing an ever-increasing surplus of food, clothing, and manufactured goods, and it had grown from a poor, underdeveloped nation to become the world's eighth largest market economy. It looked as though Brazil had worked an economic miracle. But skyrocketing interest rates and the steep rise in oil prices forced the country to borrow heavily to pay for oil imports, and economic mismanagement eventually led to gyrating inflation rates and economic stagnation.

Although part of the Third World debt was borrowed from governments and international agencies like the World Bank and International Monetary Fund, the majority was borrowed from banks in North America, Japan, and Western Europe. Those borrowing the money were primarily Third World governments or government-guaranteed enterprises. Of the $100 billion owed by Mexico at the end of the 1980s, for example, 70 percent was owed to foreign commercial banks and 30 percent to foreign governments and agencies. The major borrower was the Mexican government, which owed over half of the country's debt in the form of medium- and long-term loans. The remaining short-term debt was owed by both the government and the private sector.

Not all Third World debt is in U.S. dollars, but the various loans in Swiss francs, German marks, British pounds, and other currencies are usually translated into dollars to make the debt figures easier to understand.

54. WHAT CAUSED THE INTERNATIONAL DEBT CRISIS?

I F YOU OWE the bank a small amount of money and you can't pay it, then you are in trouble. However, if you owe the bank an enormous amount of money and you can't pay it, then the bank is in trouble.

By the end of the 1980s, European and American banks that had made large loans to the Third World were in big trouble. Countries such as Argentina, Brazil, and Mexico just could not pay the money back. In many cases, the debtor countries could not even afford to pay the interest on their outstanding loans. And some of the American creditor banks did not have enough capital and reserves to cover these nonperforming loans.

The developing countries had gambled in the 1970s and borrowed billions of dollars from Japanese and Western banks, hoping to grow their way out of poverty. But the gamble failed. By the 1980s, the debtor countries of the Third World found themselves confronted with the scissors effect of soaring interest rates and an economic slump in the developed countries, reducing worldwide demand and lowering inflation. The prices of commodities such as coffee and sugar fell sharply, reducing many developing countries' export earnings. Debtor countries were forced to borrow even more money to pay for the increased cost of oil and debt payments.

Although some of the original loans had been used to line the pockets of government officials and businessmen, much of the money was actually spent on valuable infrastructure projects like electricity systems and roads. But the tragedy of the debt crisis is that the majority of the Third World's debt was generated on the back of the debt itself. The high interest payments of the 1980s, largely caused by the U.S.

Federal Reserve's battle against inflation, had to be paid for with increased borrowing as the debtor countries of the Third World refused to admit that their gamble was failing.

Brazil, for example, had managed to keep its economy alive during the 1980s despite the huge interest payments it had to make to service its debt. It exported a wide range of goods, ranging from coffee and airplanes to tanks and shoes, racking up annual trade surpluses of ten to twenty billion U.S. dollars, the third highest trade surplus in the world after Japan and West Germany. But most of these earnings were sent abroad just to pay the interest on more than $100 billion of debt, the highest in the developing world. Funds were being transferred abroad instead of invested into the weakening Brazilian economy.

Faced with the impossibility of more foreign loans, the Brazilian government was forced to start looking for funds within the country. This was done by issuing *domestic debt*, usually in the form of government bonds. In order to attract buyers for its bonds within Brazil, the government had to pay high interest rates, sometimes several percentage points higher than the inflation rate. For example, with local inflation at 20 percent per year, the government would pay 25 percent interest on its bonds, for a "real" interest rate of 5 percent.

Eventually, the Brazilian government was forced to issue even more debt to pay for its increased interest payments. Internal debt soared, because not enough taxes were being collected to pay for the increased government spending.

By borrowing more money on the back of the original loans, the debt problem was only getting worse. But neither the banks nor the Third World debtor countries wanted to admit that there was just no money available. Not only were the debtor countries unable to pay back the principal—the original amount borrowed—in many cases they were not even able to keep up with the interest payments. The principal and interest payments on the loans had built up like a snowball rolling downhill, and the borrowers and the banks of the world found themselves in trouble.

55. WHAT IS HYPERINFLATION?

D URING A PERIOD of hyperinflation in Argentina, when the currency was losing its value at an alarming rate, it was joked that it was cheaper to take a taxi than a bus, because the bus ride was paid for at the beginning, when the currency was still worth something, while the taxi ride was paid for at the end after the currency had already lost its value.

Hyperinflation—an explosion in the prices of goods and services—is a symptom of an economy out of control. Hyperinflation has occurred all over the world: in Germany between the two world wars, and later in Israel and parts of Eastern Europe. But it has been most widespread in the debtor countries of Latin America, where it resulted primarily from government policies that attempt to satisfy political demands without increasing taxes.

When a profligate government finances spending by increased borrowing or by simply printing new currency, prices will increase as the new money enters the economy. The expectation of runaway inflation fuels the fires of hyperinflation. Eventually this wage and price spiral takes on a life of its own: prices rise, leading to a demand for increased wages, which results in higher prices. Imagine buying goods for a home or factory, or playing *The Price is Right,* when prices are increasing 200 percent a month. Even winning the lottery may not help when a million or a billion pesos does not even pay for next month's rent.

The rising prices of hyperinflation end up hurting the poor people most, because their day-to-day expenses consume a significantly higher percentage of their total income. Some countries try to index salaries and social service payments to keep up with inflation, but salaries and social service payments rarely keep pace with the increase in prices, and purchasing power declines. Even though a salary is increased in nominal terms, what the salary will actually buy—its real value—can decline. Hyperinflation especially hurts those on fixed incomes such as old-age pensions: when there are no cost-of-living increases, stipends can become virtually worthless.

Governments often refuse to take tough economic action against hyperinflation because they fear the political consequences of austerity plans or increased taxes. In order to keep large state work forces satisfied, for example, governments borrow money to keep from closing inefficient state industries or reduce bloated bureaucracies. Overburdened governments usually keep the economy going by increasing the money supply even further, issuing more government debt or printing even more money. As the government loses control of the economy, the vicious circle of wage and price increases spins out of control.

56. WHO IS HURT MOST BY ECONOMIC AUSTERITY PLANS?

TO SOLVE THE Third World's economic problems, many banks and governments in the wealthy countries take the view that a country in trouble should be treated as one solid entity, with its rich and poor populations sharing the burden of economic austerity plans. The problem is that many Third World countries are made up of a small rich elite and an enormous underclass, with the rich elite making the economic decisions, leaving the poor to suffer the consequences.

When Third World governments decide to tighten their belts, the burden is often shifted from the borrowing elites onto the poor, most of whom never benefited from the money lent to Third World businesses and governments and yet are asked to shoulder the burden of paying for it.

Many debtor countries, with the prodding of international aid organizations such as the International Monetary Fund, have developed *structural adjustment* plans to manage their debt problems. Under most of these plans, the debtor country tries to reduce its domestic consumption of goods such as shoes or orange juice in order to export more. The increased exports are then used to earn the foreign currency to pay the outstanding debt.

In many of the debtor countries, however, the goods that are restricted are often those that are the most important for a poor person's daily survival. Many economic austerity plans, for example, reduce government subsidies for consumer products such as food and transportation, making them more expensive. Governments also remove price controls, allowing the prices for products to rise along with inflation. At the same time, a cap is put on wages, which produces an effective wage cut. If the currency is devalued, it becomes even more expensive to import basic commodities like wheat and fuel.

Economic restructuring plans, such as those imposed by the International Monetary Fund, may eventually improve life for the people of debt-ridden economies. But it is especially difficult for the poor to bear the short-term burdens of economic austerity. Since many of the Third World poor are already living at subsistence levels, an increase in the cost of essential goods is a much bigger burden for them than for the wealthy. It is not very difficult to go without a new refrigerator—but it is very difficult to go without the food to put in it.

57. WHAT CAN BE DONE TO PROMOTE
THIRD WORLD DEVELOPMENT?

ECONOMIC GROWTH cannot possibly solve all the problems facing the billions of poor and undernourished people in the Third World, but because of rapid population growth, their problems would almost certainly get worse without it.

In order to provide the basic food, clothing, and shelter for their citizens, the underdeveloped Third World countries need to stimulate their stagnating economies caught in a vicious circle of low growth and declining export earnings. One of the first steps in encouraging development would be to reduce the Third World's debt and supply additional funds to revive their moribund economies. One such plan was formulated in the 1980s by U.S. Treasury secretary Nicholas Brady, who called for the commercial banks to forgive part of the debt owed to them and to increase new lending. The basic goal of the Brady plan was to encourage economic growth in the Third World.

The Brady plan also called upon the world's major development banks and funds, such as the World Bank and the International Monetary Fund, to provide substantial "project loans" to rebuild the infrastructure in the Third World. In addition, continued bank lending in the form of "adjustment loans" would help with the payment of interest and principal on previous loans. Basically, the Brady plan called for a net transfer of funds back to the developing countries.

Another way to promote Third World development is to increase development funds provided by regional development banks with the backing of the developed countries. The Inter-American Development Bank, for example, was set up to provide low-interest loans to developing countries in the Western Hemisphere. In this way, funds from wealthy countries can be channeled to less-developed nations in the form of "development loans."

Wealthy creditor governments also have the option of writing off their debt, accepting that it will never be repaid. France, for example, decided in the 1980s that most of its development loans to African countries need not be repaid, in an effort to encourage further economic growth in the region.

In order to provide further assistance to Third World debtors, the world's wealthy countries can also work through specialized organizations such as the Lomé Convention, which channels development aid from the European Community to poor Third World countries, and the Paris Club, which helps governments of debtor nations "reschedule" or delay repayment of their loans until their economies are in better shape.

58. HOW CAN INTERNATIONAL ECONOMIC COOPERATION BE ENCOURAGED?

JUST AS the United Nations Security Council can be used to solve the world's military and political disputes, many of the problems arising from global trade and investment can be solved through the assistance of international groups or organizations.

One of the most active groups in formulating common economic goals is the Organization for Economic Co-Operation and Development (OECD). In addition to providing statistics and documents on almost all aspects of the international economy, the OECD serves as a forum for discussions and coordination of economic policy. The OECD, headquartered in Paris, brings together the richest members of the world economy, including most of the Western European countries, the United States, Canada, Japan, Australia, and New Zealand. This group of twenty-four OECD countries has sometimes been referred to simply as "G-24."

International economic cooperation has also been encouraged through periodic economic summits, including the "G-7" summit of the world's seven most powerful economies: the United States, Japan, Germany, Italy, Britain, France, and Canada. The G-7 summit began as a purely economic forum but expanded quickly to cover a wide variety of international economic and political issues such as Eastern European economic reform and protection of the environment.

Having political leaders meet to discuss economic issues is essential to world peace because the world's economic problems are, in fact, inseparable from military and political conflicts, and vice versa. Iraq's decision to invade Kuwait, for example, leading to the gulf war in 1991, was principally motivated by economic factors: access to Kuwait's oil fields and shipping facilities.

The security of the world depends on the creation of strong and stable economies. Complex international issues like global pollution, trade imbalances, and the Third World debt cannot always be resolved by countries acting unilaterally, but often depend on nations working together through international groups and agencies.

59. HOW CAN TRADE WARS BE AVOIDED?

ALTHOUGH A trade war is not the same as a military war, in both cases people suffer, including those the trade war was meant to protect in the first place.

Every country wants access to the world's markets, but at times it may seem easier to close borders rather than to face strong foreign competition. When a country raises trade barriers, it can quickly turn into a trade war, as other countries around the world retaliate with trade barriers of their own. Solving trade disputes is critical, because sometimes they may escalate into global economic battles or all-out military conflict.

The closest thing the world has to a set of laws governing trade is called GATT, the General Agreement on Tariffs and Trade. More than just an agreement, GATT is an organization located on the shores of Lake Geneva in Switzerland. It has more than one hundred members, including most of the world's industrialized countries. GATT is charged with overseeing international trade among member states and provides a forum for resolving disputes. Trade agreements, such as the Uruguay Round, are periodically organized by GATT to define and encourage international trade on a worldwide basis.

In a way, GATT acts as a policeman to keep countries from erecting trade barriers such as quotas or tariffs on imports. Even though no country can be forced to comply with a GATT decision, the threat of economic retaliation by other trading nations can usually force GATT member countries to play by the rules of the world economy.

Although it is a policeman without a gun, GATT has been fairly successful in reducing trade barriers. For example, when Japan and the United States decided at the end of the 1980s to reduce their massive trade imbalances, much of the work was done through GATT, eventually succeeding in reducing barriers until they affected less than 5 percent of the goods traded.

If countries choose not to use the multilateral services of GATT to solve trade disputes, they can attempt to meet with their opponents one-on-one and work out some sort of bilateral agreement. Failing this, a country may decide to act unilaterally. Unfortunately, by erecting their own trade barriers, most countries end up cutting themselves off from the world, further reducing trade and economic growth.

60. WHAT ARE THE REGIONAL DEVELOPMENT

BANKS?

WHEN A neighborhood bank decides to provide extra loans to build local homes and businesses, the whole community usually benefits from the increased economic activity. In the same way, the world's *regional development banks* provide development funds for needy countries. These development loans serve to channel funds from the rich countries to the "have-nots."

Development banks are not ordinary profit-oriented banks; they do not take traditional deposits but are funded by large capital commitments and loans from the developed countries such as the United States, Japan, and Switzerland. These funds are then lent at a low rate of interest to needy countries. Development bank loans often include a grace period of two to seven years before the borrower starts to pay back the original amount borrowed, called the *principal*. This provides time for a project, a hydroelectric dam for example, to start making money before the principal payments begin.

The biggest of the regional development banks is the Inter-American Development Bank (IADB), based in Washington, D.C. Funded primarily by countries in the Western Hemisphere, the IADB provides loans for development projects in the poor countries of Latin America.

The Asian Development Bank (ADB) was set up in 1966 to foster economic growth in Asia and the Pacific region. Headquartered in the Philippines, the ADB provides most of its loans for agricultural projects in countries such as Indonesia, the Philippines, Pakistan, and Thailand.

The African Development Bank (AfDB), the smallest of the development banks, is based in Abidjan in the Ivory Coast. Its loans are used mainly for public utilities, transportation, and agricultural projects in the poorest regions of Africa.

The European Investment Bank (EIB) provides funds for local projects in Western Europe, such as the Channel tunnel. Following the decision of the Eastern European countries to enter the free-market economy, the European Bank for Reconstruction and Development (EBRD) was set up in London in 1990 to provide massive amounts of development aid to countries such as Poland, Hungary, Czechoslovakia, Estonia, Latvia, and Lithuania.

61. WHAT ARE THE WORLD BANK AND THE IMF?

WHILE REFORMING Poland's debt-ridden centrally planned economy at the end of the 1980s, the Solidarity government received many large loans from the West, including development loans and assistance from the World Bank and the International Monetary Fund. These "sister" institutions, located across the street from each other in Washington, D.C., serve many roles, including supervising the world economy and providing "last resort" assistance to economies in need.

The International Bank for Reconstruction and Development (IBRD), referred to as the World Bank, provides development aid to the world's poor and underdeveloped countries. The International Monetary Fund (IMF), concentrates on providing advice and temporary funds for countries with economic difficulties.

The major role of the World Bank, the world's biggest development bank, is to provide a helping hand to countries in need. Its first activity, after being set up in Washington, D.C., in 1945, was to channel funds from the United States and other nations into rebuilding Europe after World War II. For example, its first loans were used to rebuild war-torn Holland, Denmark, and France. The World Bank now provides most of its loans to countries in the Third World, and receives a significant portion of its funding from the now wealthy nations it was initially designed to assist.

Like the regional development banks, the World Bank receives its funds from its rich member countries, which in turn provide it with the credit to borrow cheaply on the world's capital markets. This allows the World Bank to provide these funds at extremely favorable rates to needy countries.

In order to address the underlying causes of poverty in many developing nations, the World Bank often relies on the International Monetary Fund to encourage debtor countries to make difficult economic reforms. The IMF, located across the street from the World Bank in Washington, D.C., is also funded by wealthy member countries such as Japan, France, and the United States. It serves to supervise the international monetary system and acts as a safety net for economies in trouble.

Like a doctor called in at the last minute, the IMF is often asked to resuscitate ailing economies. This "structural adjustment" process is a crucial first step before receiving development assistance from other sources. Acceptance of an IMF plan is usually seen as a sign that a nation is prepared to seriously address its economic ills, paving the way for long-term funding from the World Bank and other sources.

The economic medicine prescribed by the IMF is often painful. For example, it often calls for debtor governments to reduce subsidies to failing state industries and insists on strict anti-inflationary measures such as increasing the prices of basic goods and services. During the difficult restructuring processes, the IMF often provides temporary "standby" loans to keep the country afloat until more long-term funding can be arranged.

62. HOW IS CORRUPTION PART OF THE WORLD ECONOMY?

FOR BUSINESSES and governments in many countries around the world, corruption is a way of life. Corruption takes all forms: without some sort of bribery, government officials in many countries will not approve imports or exports; company presidents want money deposited into secret Swiss bank accounts before signing any contracts; and military officers refuse to pay for shipments of arms without a monetary "present."

Those who accept these payoffs point out that their salaries are purposefully low because it is assumed that their income will be supplemented by bribes, just as a waiter in a restaurant will accept a lower salary knowing that a large portion of the day's income will come from tips.

For people from relatively honest countries, it often seems impossible to compete abroad without getting dirty. One way of avoiding corruption is for relatively honest countries to make laws clearly prohibiting their citizens from engaging in bribery in their business dealings abroad. If foreigners know that certain people are prohibited from providing bribes by their home country, they often will not ask for one. The United States, for example, clearly prohibits international bribery through the Foreign Corrupt Practices Act.

Antibribery laws do not necessarily reduce a country's competitiveness on the international markets. In many cases, firms doing business abroad can avoid bribery by working more closely with local partners who have already established business and family ties within the local community. These local partnerships may actually provide additional business expertise and succeed in opening doors that bribery may not have opened at all.

63. WHAT IS MONEY LAUNDERING?

THE WORLD'S criminals need to periodically recycle their "dirty money" so that it can be used in the economy at large without anyone knowing about its illegal past.

A money laundering scheme is the process that turns large sums of illegally earned funds into "respectable" money. A drug dealer, for example, may end a day's work with a large amount of cash that needs to be deposited or otherwise spent. Since there is a limit to the number of luxury automobiles and condominiums a drug dealer can effectively use or buy without creating suspicion, illicit earnings need to be put into a bank, to be available for future use.

The key to any money laundering scheme is to get the money into legitimate bank accounts without alerting law-enforcement officials to the money's illicit past. Once the money is in a legitimate account, it can be transferred around the world without interference from the authorities.

International bank transfers are just electronic messages, from one bank to another, that instruct banks to put money from one account into another. The sheer size of these international computerized transfers, often exceeding $1 trillion per day, makes them difficult to control. The illegal transfers disappear in a sea of legal ones.

One popular money-laundering practice is to make hundreds of small deposits to avoid having large deposits reported to law-enforcement agencies. Another alternative is to mix illegal deposits with legal ones, channeling illegally earned money through legitimate businesses that use banks for processing large amounts of legally earned deposits. A restaurant that does not accept credit cards, for example, deposits a large amount of cash each day in banks. These transfers can then serve as a cover for deposits of illicit funds.

The currency of choice for most drug-related and other illegal transactions is the U.S. dollar. This partly explains why more than half of the U.S. greenbacks printed cannot be found anywhere in the American economy. Drug lords in the Far East, underground traders in Eastern Europe, and black market currency dealers in Latin America all make use of the U.S. dollar for their illegal activities.

The U.S. dollar, mainly twenty- and hundred-dollar bills, came into use as an underground currency because of its liquidity: it can be exchanged almost anywhere in the world without raising suspicion. Because of the size and stability of the U.S. economy, the U.S. dollar has become the preferred currency for most players in the underground economies of the world.

64. HOW DOES A SWISS BANK ACCOUNT WORK?

S WITZERLAND IS one of the few countries in the world that guarantees, by law, the secrecy of its bank accounts. As long as the client of a Swiss bank has not done anything that is considered illegal in Switzerland, the bank will not reveal the client's identity to anyone.

During World War II, for example, many families from war-torn Germany, Italy, and France were able to keep their savings secure by putting them in Swiss banks. Many Europeans still consider having a bank account in Zurich, Basel, Lugano, or Geneva to be a sign of financial security.

Opening a legal, numbered Swiss bank account is still relatively easy to do, usually involving nothing more than going to Switzerland, filling out a few forms, and making a deposit. Swiss bankers are known to be dependable, trustworthy, and, above all, discreet. These qualities have made Switzerland one of the world's banking centers. But they have also made Switzerland a center for money laundering.

Swiss bank accounts are useful for money-laundering schemes because once money passes through a respectable Swiss bank, it is accepted anywhere in the world. When several Swiss banks were found to be facilitating the activities of international drug traffickers in the 1980s, the Swiss authorities finally decided to break open several secret accounts that were linked to illegal activities abroad.

Most people holding Swiss bank accounts, however, do not use them to launder illegally earned money. They merely want their legally earned funds to be safe and free from government control and taxes at home. Swiss bankers do not reveal the accounts of clients accused of avoiding taxes in their home country, since tax evasion is not considered to be "illegal" in Switzerland: it is only a civil, not a criminal offense.

Foreigners—as long as they break no Swiss laws—can keep their money in Swiss bank accounts without fear. This guarantee of secrecy can be used by many unscrupulous people for a wide variety of shady international activities. In the case of the Iran-contra scandals during the 1980s, for example, the secret deals between America's CIA and the Iranian arms merchants were paid for in part with money deposited by CIA agents at banks in Switzerland.

Philippine dictator Ferdinand Marcos had also deposited large sums of illegally acquired funds in Swiss banks during the 1970s and 1980s. When he was deposed, the Philippine government called for the return of these funds, which was agreed to by the Swiss authorities. After several abuses of Swiss banking secrecy, the Swiss authorities announced that they would be ready to open any accounts revealed to be linked to illegal international activity.

65. WHAT IS A TAX HAVEN?

THE TERM *tax haven* usually conjures up images of palm trees and shady criminals sitting around swimming pools drinking banana daiquiris.

The purpose of a tax haven, however, is not to facilitate illegal international activities but to provide a low-tax environment to attract individuals and businesses to otherwise overlooked economic centers. The most popular tax havens are found on islands in the Caribbean and the Pacific, or in small countries in Europe and Central America.

Many small states, such as the Cayman Islands or the Isle of Man, require little or no taxes from the foreigners who come there to set up operations. It is a lucrative opportunity that some companies and individuals do not want to pass up. Just as many U.S. companies choose to register their headquarters in Delaware to take advantage of lower taxes and favorable legal requirements, many international companies set up subsidiaries on small islands like those of the Netherlands Antilles to benefit from favorable international regulations and tax rates.

Many companies from Europe and North America have also used subsidiaries in the Netherlands Antilles to issue bonds in the Eurobond market. These "offshore" operations have allowed many companies to raise funds in the international capital markets with a minimum of regulations and taxes.

Some individuals also prefer the anonymity of setting up companies in tax havens. They can then choose whether or not to report the income booked through these offshore companies to their home country. Even though this is illegal in their home country, it is not necessarily illegal in the tax haven itself.

Although tax havens do attract some illegal operations, such as money laundering, most activity in the world's tax havens fully complies with international laws and regulations.

66. HOW DO INTERNATIONAL CRIMINALS

ESCAPE PROSECUTION?

THE MASTERMIND of Britain's famous Briggs train robbery was able to escape from the scene of the crime and flee to Rio, knowing that he could live in freedom. The British authorities were helpless to act because there was no treaty between Britain and Brazil requiring the transfer of such criminals. Although Brazil does extradite some criminals to face trial for their criminal activities abroad, it is one of many countries in the world economy that does not extradite all criminals for all crimes.

International criminals rarely get away with murder, which is clearly illegal in every country in the world. Most international drug traffickers, for example, are extraditable, and many countries such as Colombia and Mexico have sent drug traffickers to face prosecution in the United States. They have signed joint extradition treaties that cover the illegal trade of narcotics.

But different laws in different countries can hinder authorities from tracking down and prosecuting criminals who make their living in the interlinked global economy. What is perfectly legal in one country—buying and selling foreign currencies, for example—may be strictly prohibited in another. When one country attempts to extradite accused criminals from foreign hideaways, their pleas may fall on deaf ears. Authorities abroad are usually reluctant to extradite people accused of activities they do not consider to be a criminal offense.

Tax evasion, for example, is severely punished in the United States, but it is not considered to be an extraditable offense in Switzerland. An American living in Switzerland who is accused of U.S. tax evasion—a civil rather than a criminal offense in Switzerland—would not normally be extradited.

Prosecuting international criminals is most difficult when the laws they are accused of breaking at home do not even exist abroad. While insider stock trading is illegal in some countries, in Britain and the United States for example, it is accepted as a smart business practice in others. Hong Kong, for instance, has often allowed those lucky enough to be "in the know" to trade on information that is not available to the general public. As long as countries have different customs and laws, some international criminals will always be able to escape prosecution.

67. WHAT ARE BLACK MARKETS?

I LLEGAL OR semilegal goods and services, ranging from endangered animals and foreign currencies to prostitution and drugs, are traded every day on the world's black markets.

In those countries with currency restrictions, for example, black market currency exchanges have flourished. When the official rate is out of sync with the real value of a currency, people start trading outside the official market. In Brazil, this was tolerated to the point that the black market rates were published as parallel exchange rates in the newspapers.

The world economy is also full of semilegal or "gray market" activities such as transfers and deposits of legally earned but undeclared funds that have to be hidden from the authorities at home. For example, normally law-abiding Italian, French, and Latin American citizens have often transferred money to bank accounts abroad during periods of domestic economic instability and exchange restrictions.

The formation of a shadow economy, where "gray money" transfers need to be kept hidden even though they are legal, has opened the door to a wide variety of abuses. In the United States and Europe, for example, a large amount of illegally earned drug or organized crime money finds its way into the gray economy, where it is hidden among the large quantities of legal money in the world economy that require a certain amount of secrecy. The volume of gray money transfers, estimated to be over $1 trillion per year, more than the GDP of most countries, is so big that regulators cannot monitor it all. The "black" money gets lost in the sea of gray money transfers.

68. HOW IS THE ENVIRONMENT AFFECTED BY THE WORLD ECONOMY?

ALTHOUGH IT is not always obvious, almost every one of the world's man-made environmental problems is a direct result of an economic decision. Pollution, for example, exists because it is more expensive for countries and companies to clean up pollutants than it is to dump them into the water and the air.

No one wants to pollute, but environmental protection, like all other economic decisions, involves an economic trade-off. Companies, countries, and even consumers must decide how much they are ready to pay to keep the environment clean and healthy. This decision is, essentially, an economic one.

Industrial nations have often treated the world and its resources as if they were disposable commodities. They were ignoring a basic economic concept: all factors of production—whether land, labor, or air—are scarce commodities and have a price that has to be factored into all business and economic decisions. Clean air and water, once thought of as being limitless, have been rapidly depleted by growing populations and rampant industrial development, and need to be treated like any other scarce resource.

Although governments and consumer groups play an important role in protecting the environment, in the end it is more often the sustained pressure of economic incentives that forces companies and governments to change environmentally unsound practices and policies. When a company is forced to pay for its pollution, for example, it will think twice before discharging its waste into the air and water. And when a government is forced to include the depletion of natural resources in its calculation of total economic activity—creating an "environmental GDP," for example—it may think twice about wasting precious forests and mineral deposits.

Like all sectors of the world economy, environmental protection is not limited by national barriers. What one country does to alter the environment has an effect on others. Whether it is deforestation, depletion of the ozone layer, or dumping of radioactive waste in the ocean, every major issue of environmental pollution is international in nature.

Environmental protection and awareness can by no means be confined to the modern industrial economies. The people of the Third World are especially affected by issues such as global warming and deforestation. The low-lying regions of Bangladesh, for example, would be the first hit by any rise in the level of the world's oceans as a result of global warming. Furthermore, the costs of protecting the environment are especially high for the developing countries where many natural resources have been depleted and vast areas have been polluted in the drive for economic growth.

A healthy environment need not be incompatible with a prosperous economy. Indeed, some of the world's most destructive pollution has occurred in economically backward countries, such as in the former Soviet bloc of Eastern Europe. In contrast, some of the world's cleanest air and water can be found in advanced industrial economies such as in Canada and Sweden. By looking at environmental issues from an international perspective it becomes clear that protecting the environment is the only way for the world to sustain healthy economic growth in the years to come.

69. WHAT ARE POLLUTION RIGHTS?

ONE OF the most difficult problems facing the world economy is how to increase the standard of living for growing populations without destroying the environment. Several countries, including the United States, have turned to an innovative system limiting total pollution in any given area and then allowing local industries and other companies to buy and sell *pollution rights* among themselves.

Many environmental groups have come to support such systems because they come as close as possible to solving two seemingly irreconcilable goals: economic growth and a clean environment. The key to the pollution rights plan is to induce companies and other polluters to reduce their output of emissions in the most efficient way possible.

Faced with the difficult task of reducing economic activity in order to reduce pollution, many countries simply cannot afford to shut down plants producing essential food, shelter, and clothing for their people. Although it may seem fair to force everyone to reduce pollution equally by putting limits on each polluter's output, under such systems governments end up giving the "right to pollute" to all producers, whether or not they are efficient and useful to the economy at large.

Instead of requiring all polluters to reduce their output, the pollution rights plan recognizes that there are differences between polluters: some should go out of business, while others should be allowed to grow to provide jobs and products for an expanding economy. In a free-market system, there is an efficient way of telling the "good" from the "bad" polluters: the invisible hand of the marketplace. Those companies that should not be polluting are the inefficient ones that provide the least number of jobs and products for the economy. The goal of the pollution rights plan is to induce these "bad" polluters to go out of business or at least reduce their activities.

An efficiently run wheelchair factory, for example, will produce less pollution per product than an inefficient one. Under a traditional antipollution plan, a government would limit the production at both plants, allowing both the inefficient factory and the efficient factory to continue producing and polluting at lower levels. By forcing all factories to reduce pollution levels equally, a government gives a pollution "right" to all, whether they are producing efficiently or not.

If this "right" could be sold, an inefficient producer could be induced to reduce its pollution for a fee: it is paid by the efficient company to reduce its activities in exchange for a cash payment. The efficient company can then use these pollution rights to increase production. There is no increase in the total amount of pollution: the pollution rights are simply transferred from one enterprise to another.

The same principle applies to international pollution. What goes into the air above Chicago may come down as acid rain in Quebec. And what goes into the water in Basel, Switzerland, can end up polluting the North Sea. Pollution knows no national boundaries, and international agreements can limit the total amount of pollution and then use a pollution rights barter to distribute the rights throughout the world economy.

No one country or company has a right to pollute, but if a limited amount of pollution is allowed, it is to everybody's benefit to distribute the pollution rights in a way that is least harmful to the economy at large. The goal in a pollution rights barter is not to pollute more, but to *produce* more efficiently with a limited amount of environmental pollution.

In some cases, the total amount of pollution can actually be reduced. A city government or an interested environmental group, for example, could buy the pollution rights from an inefficient factory and decide not to use them, putting them away in a drawer, reducing the overall level of pollution with a minimum of disruption to efficient economic production.

70. WHAT IS A DEBT-FOR-NATURE SWAP?

DEBT-FOR-NATURE SWAPS allow banks, environmental groups, and debtor countries to join together to protect a valuable part of the environment such as a forest or a wildlife refuge.

Since many poor countries do not even have the financial resources to repay their foreign loans, it is difficult to get them to spend money on "luxuries" such as nature parks or wildlife preserves. Environmental protection groups, however, have devised an ingenious method for getting a poor debtor country such as Colombia or Peru to protect its natural heritage: they pay off the poor country's debt in exchange for a commitment to protect ecologically valuable land such as forests, wetlands, or regions rich in wildlife.

In the world financial markets, many Third World loans are sold at a discount to their original face value because no one expects poor debtor countries to repay all of their debt. Debt, like any other financial instrument, can be bought and sold on the open market. A bank, for example, can sell a loan to another bank in the same way someone sells a bond or another IOU. The purchaser of a loan expects to get paid back by the original borrower. Some of the doubtful loans to Third World countries, however, sell for as little as 10 percent of their original face value. An environmental group can therefore buy a $100 million doubtful loan for as little as $10 million.

Once an environmental group uses its funds to purchase this debt on the open market at a fraction of its original value, it gives the debt back to the debtor country—in effect "paying it off" or canceling it—in exchange for environmental concessions. Environmental groups prefer debt-for-nature swaps because they get more bang for their buck—buying the loans from the creditor banks for a lot less money than they are officially worth.

All parties to a debt-for-nature swap are able to benefit in some way. The debtor country ends up with a nature park and a reduction in debt. International banks are happy to see their debt exposure reduced even if it means getting only a part of their money back. And the environmental group has been able to preserve an ecologically important part of the world for future generations.

71. HOW CAN ECONOMIC SANCTIONS AND INCENTIVES BE USED TO PROTECT THE ENVIRONMENT?

FROM THE endangered mountain gorillas of Africa to the vanishing trees and plants of the Amazon rain forest, natural resources around the world can be given new hope through economic sanctions and incentives. For example, once it is shown that precious forests and wildlife are worth more alive than dead, people will finally begin to change their environmentally—and economically—destructive behavior.

Until recently, the destruction of forests, rivers, and wildlife around the world has often been carried out in the name of economic progress. Many companies and governments were not aware of the fact that long-term economic growth is essentially based on renewable resources and on a healthy environment.

The Amazon rain forest, for example, was being destroyed at an alarming rate during the 1980s largely because of misguided economic policy. Poorly conceived tax laws in Brazil provided an incentive for farmers to move into the Amazon and burn large areas of the rain forest for crops or cattle grazing. These policies had questionable economic value and disastrous environmental consequences, including further global warming from the sudden release of large quantities of carbon dioxide into the atmosphere.

Although at first Brazil claimed national sovereignty over its rain forests, the international outcry over the wholesale destruction of the Amazon forced the Brazilian government to reconsider its environmentally harmful policies. The result was a dramatic curb in the amount of rain forest being destroyed. Although a country's environmentally destructive actions can be changed in the short term by applying international political pressure, long-term changes can be brought about only by making a country aware of the economic value of preserving its natural resources.

By providing economic incentives such as tourist income or exports of renewable products, countries begin to see the true value of preserving precious natural resources. Instead of slaughtering elephant herds or mountain gorillas, for example, a country can create wildlife refuges to stimulate tourism. And by periodically harvesting the fruits, nuts, and plants found in the rain forests, countries can earn valuable foreign exchange. The income from medicinal and food exports from a living rain forest can often surpass the questionable profit of burning the trees. And, in the end, the whole world breathes a lot easier.

Another effective way of forcing a government or a company to change environmentally harmful practices is to threaten economic sanctions such as boycotts and trade restrictions. The threat of a consumer boycott of the offending company's goods on the world markets, for example, can be quite effective because it provides the most powerful economic incentive around: the loss of profits. For example, the destructive practice of drift-net fishing, needlessly killing many porpoises, was changed only after consumers threatened to boycott the tuna of the offending companies.

Governments can also impose trade restrictions, such as embargoes that prohibit the import of goods from countries with environmentally harmful practices. Trade restrictions, however, often end up provoking the targeted country into erecting trade barriers of its own, ultimately hurting all people concerned. But when a number of nations band together to send a clear message, threats of retaliation often lose their punch.

International agreements on protecting the environment can also be effective in altering environmentally unsound practices, but only if they are backed up by the political and economic pressure of the countries involved. Agreements reached at the United Nations, for example, are especially effective when they are in the form of a General Assembly resolution, voted for by all of the member countries. Although these resolutions are usually nonbinding, direct enforcement is unnecessary if broad worldwide support for them can be obtained.

The best solution, however, is often found in international conferences where all nations concerned can sit down and reach some form of a negotiated settlement. In many ways, the environment's future depends on rational economic growth managed through international cooperation.

GLOSSARY

T HIS LIST is meant to provide a convenient reference for words from the world economy that pop up during the course of a conversation or in the daily news. "What is a current account?" "What is a leveraged buyout?" "What is perestroika?" These are questions that we may have asked ourselves more than once. Even after finding the answer, we may need to refresh our memories several weeks later when the term comes up again.

This list is intended to be as light and informative as possible, and can be returned to time and time again.

American Depository Receipt (ADR). To make things easy for American investors who want to buy shares of a foreign company, an American bank buys the shares and holds them on deposit. It issues a receipt, called an ADR, that gives the American the right to the foreign shares and the dividends, which are paid in U.S. dollars. The majority of ADRs are traded on over-the-counter markets.

Arbitrage. When there are price differences for the same product in different markets, an arbitrager will buy large quantities in the cheap market and sell them in the expensive one. The practice of arbitrage is simple and has been used for centuries to make profits and keep the markets efficient. Recently, takeover specialists have used the techniques of arbitrage to buy shares of undervalued companies in order to resell them at a higher price when the companies have been restructured.

Asset. On a balance sheet, assets are positives, liabilities are negatives.

The assets of most companies include financial assets such as cash and securities, fixed assets such as buildings and machinery, and nontangible assets such as goodwill, brand names, patents, and copyrights.

Asset stripping. When an undervalued company is acquired, its assets can be sold in pieces to make more money than it cost to acquire the whole company. Asset stripping is a key factor in the takeover game, where the proceeds from assets are used to pay off the debt incurred when acquiring the company.

Balance of payments. A country's balance of payments measures its total international trade in goods, services, and money. It is a "balance" because each country's transfer of goods and services is balanced by an equal transfer of money in the opposite direction. For example, a country with an export surplus receives money for the goods and services it sends abroad: the trade in goods and services, measured by the current account, is balanced by transfers of money, measured by the capital account.

Balance sheet. A balance sheet lists all of the company's assets and liabilities. This provides a snapshot of the company's health at a given point in time. When the company has more assets than liabilities, the stockholders are happy. Their share, the difference between assets and liabilities, is called shareholders' equity.

Bankruptcy. When a company can't pay its debts, it declares bankruptcy. In some countries, bankrupt companies are given an opportunity to restructure in order to pay off their creditors. This is called Chapter Eleven in the United States and receivership in Britain. If the company can find no other solution, it is liquidated. Its assets are then sold to pay as many of the creditors as possible.

Barter. Exchanging one good for another, barter allows traders to avoid the problems of unconvertible currencies. In most developed countries barter is unnecessary because it is much easier to use money to buy and sell goods. But in many countries with artificially fixed exchange rates, the local currency cannot be converted on the international markets. Barter is often the only alternative for anyone wanting to do business in countries short of hard currencies such as U.S. dollars and German marks.

Basis point. A hundred of these make one percentage point. Bond markets have gotten so finely tuned that it is no longer enough to talk about yields going up a quarter or a sixteenth of a percent. Yields can move by as little as a hundredth of a percent, or one basis point. A quarter percent rise in a bond's yield is twenty-five basis points.

Bear market/bull market. A bear, growling and pessimistic, is used to describe a declining market. A bull, charging ahead, symbolizes optimism and a rising market.

Bearer bond. Bearer bonds are the ultimate transferable security. International spies and villains like to get paid with bearer bonds because they can be cashed with no questions asked. Most international securities are issued in bearer form. There is no name on a bearer bond, and no registration. The holder of a bearer bond has the right to receive the full value of the bond at maturity, in addition to all interest payments.

Big Bang. After London's stock market was deregulated in 1986, there was supposed to be an explosion of financial and trading activity. When the Big Bang finally occurred, most of the international banks and investment houses that had bought huge stakes in the City's financial community found out that they were going to lose a lot of money because of the increased competition. Cutbacks and layoffs followed in the wake.

Bilateral trade agreements. Bilateral trade agreements are made between two countries wishing to come to some sort of understanding on how goods and services are to be traded. Many countries argue that trade barriers can be removed only when other countries are included in multilateral agreements.

Black market, black economy. Black markets will spring up wherever a good or service is prohibited or severely controlled. In some countries, black markets are tolerated with little or no police interference. In countries where currencies are artificially controlled, the black market rates usually indicate the true market price. The black economy consists of all those underground transactions that, because of their illegality, go unreported.

Bond. The ultimate IOU, a bond is a negotiable piece of paper that permits a company or a government to borrow money for a certain length of time. The pieces of paper called bonds can be bought and sold among investors. Whoever owns the bonds holds the right to receive the principal payment, when the bonds are paid back. In addition, most bonds provide an interest payment, which is a percentage of the bond's face value paid periodically. There are many kinds of bonds, including fixed-income securities, like U.S. Treasury bonds, and floating-rate notes, which have their interest rate refixed periodically. Zero-coupon bonds pay no interest rate but are sold at a discount to provide a higher return to investors when the bonds are paid back.

Bourse. The word *bourse*, which means "purse" in French, has come to mean "stock market" around the world.

Bridge loan. Bridge loans allow a borrower to receive funds for a short period of time, until more long-term loans can be arranged. The International Monetary Fund and the Bank for International Settlements usually provide bridge loans to poor countries trying to arrange loans with the World Bank and other long-term lenders. Bridge loans are paid off as soon as the long-term money is received.

Broker. Like a real estate agent who brings together buyers and sellers, a broker is a go-between who acts as an intermediary in financial transactions and usually receives a commission based on the volume of securities traded. A dealer, on the other hand, has an inventory of goods that can be sold to investors. Some investment bankers fill both roles and are called, not surprisingly, broker/dealers.

Bundesbank. Germany's central bank, the Bundesbank, is responsible for safeguarding the German currency and controlling the money supply. The Bundesbank is located in Frankfurt, Germany's financial capital.

Call option. A call option gives the right to buy something at a certain price for a certain period of time. An investor who thinks the price of a stock will go up will buy a call option. As the price of the underlying security goes up, so does the price of the call option.

International investors can buy options on such diverse instruments as stocks, commodities, futures, and foreign currencies.

Capital gains tax. A capital gain is the increase in the price of assets such as stocks or real estate. An investment in stocks, for example, will provide a capital gain if the price of the shares goes up. Capital gains are usually taxed at a different rate from other income such as interest, dividend payments, and earned income.

Capital markets. A capital market is an exchange or a group of exchanges where securities such as bonds and other long-term debt instruments are traded. In the international capital markets, U.S. Treasury bonds are the most popular investment because of their high degree of liquidity: they can be bought and sold in large size at almost any time, day or night. Most capital market trading is not done in official exchanges, but on trading floors in banks around the world that are connected electronically to form one big international market.

Cash crops/food crops. "Give a starving man a fish and he will eat for a day; give him a fishing pole and he will hunger no more." In developing countries, a farmer's crops that are used to feed only the farmer's family are called food crops. Cash crops are not consumed, but are sold to provide money to buy clothing, shelter, and other items.

Cash flow. A quick measure of the money coming into or going out of a company during a given period is called cash flow. It gives a clear idea of a company's true earnings because it excludes accounting tools, such as depreciation, that allow a company to reduce the amount of profits reported on its books in order to pay less taxes. Cash flow factors out all of the accounting tricks and looks at what a company really earned.

Centrally planned economies. In a centrally planned economy, the bureaucrats make all the decisions. The state has the authority to decide who produces what and how much. Prices and resource allocation are also decided by the central decision-making bodies. The goal is to make economic decisions more rational and equitable, but the result is often increased waste and inefficiency. Centrally planned economies are also called command economies or, simply, planned economies.

The City, Wall Street, Bahnhofstrasse. The part of London where the major banks and securities houses are located is called the City of London. The British financial community is therefore commonly referred to as simply "the City." In New York, the markets use the term "Wall Street" to describe the local financial community, while in Zurich it's the "Bahnhofstrasse" and in Tokyo the "Kabuto-cho." When Venice was the center of the world economy, the banks were all found on the Rialto. Hence, Shylock's famous line in Shakespeare's *The Merchant of Venice:* "What news on the Rialto?"

Classical economics. The basic idea of classical economics is that an economy will always move toward an equilibrium. This idea was formulated in the eighteenth and nineteenth centuries by Adam Smith, David Ricardo, and John Stuart Mill. It was thought that when too many people are looking for jobs, wages would go down until everyone becomes employed. The problem, pointed out by John Maynard Keynes in the twentieth century, is that wages rarely go down. If that is the case, classical economists may just have to "assume" full employment.

Commercial banks. A commercial bank takes deposits and makes loans. In the United States and Japan, commercial banks are prohibited by law from getting involved in investment banking activities, such as underwriting share offerings and trading stocks and bonds. The distinction is becoming blurred as commercial banks are now being allowed to move into previously prohibited investment banking territory. By the end of the 1980s, nine of the ten largest commercial banks in the world were Japanese.

Commodity. The term *commodity* is used to refer to raw materials or primary products such as gold or tea. A commodity is easily bought or sold on the world markets because it is relatively homogeneous: gold from Siberia is the same as gold from Nevada. Commodities can be traded in spot transactions for immediate delivery, with options, or by buying and selling for future delivery. Other examples of tradable commodities are wool, silver, tin, platinum, beef, oil, and, of course, the proverbial pork bellies.

The Common Market, European Community. With over 300 million consumers, Europe's Common Market has become the largest single trading bloc in the world. Formerly called the European Economic Community or EEC, and now referred to as the European Community or EC, the Common Market groups together Europe's largest and wealthiest economies.

Communism. According to Marx: "From each according to his abilities, to each according to his needs." The goal of a communist society is to achieve total equality. This utopian idea was developed during the nineteenth century by economic philosophers like Karl Marx who tried to find an alternative to the terrible abuses of the capitalist system in the early years of the Industrial Revolution. The answer, according to Marx, was a revolution of the proletariat: the workers of the world were supposed to unite and create a utopia where everyone was equal.

Comparative advantage. The theory of comparative advantage is based on the very practical idea that if a country excels in one activity, the others should not try to duplicate it. By trading goods and services, each country can concentrate on what it does best. According to the theory of comparative advantage, if one country is good at making wine, it should make wine for everyone. The others can spend their time making bread or cheese. After trading their respective products, each country can sit down to a better meal than if everything had been made in one place.

Consumer price index (CPI). In order to keep track of inflation, governments survey the prices of a "basket" of goods and services that are supposed to indicate how much an average person's expenses go up each month. The CPI is used for readjusting fixed incomes such as pensions and social security payments. The measure of each country's cost of living is based on its consumer price index, called the "retail price index" in Britain or the "cost-of-living index" elsewhere.

Convertible bond. In order to make bonds or other securities more attractive to the investor, some companies allow them to be convertible, or exchanged into something else of value, usually shares of the company. During the "life" of the bond, the owner of a convertible bond has the right, but not the obligation, to trade the bond for a fixed amount of shares. Since this is an option, the investor can only benefit—deciding, for example, to convert the bond only when the value of the company's shares are worth enough to make the conversion worthwhile.

Corporate finance. When a company or a government needs to borrow money, they usually turn to investment banks to find the best financing at the best price. What the borrowers spend on this expensive advice is often saved through reduced borrowing costs. The goal of corporate finance advisors is to find the right mix of bonds, equity, swaps, and loans that allows the borrower to secure funding at the lowest possible cost.

Correction. For those who expect the market to continue rising, an unexplained drop in prices is called a temporary market correction.

Cum, Ex. *Cum* means "with" in Latin. A bond with a warrant still attached to it is referred to as "cum." Similarly, a stock sold with the dividend still to be paid is called "cum dividend." To describe bonds or stocks for which the warrants or dividends have been removed, the word *ex,* Latin for "without," is used. A stock sold "ex," for example, has already paid its dividend to the previous owner.

Currency. A mark, a yen, a buck, or a pound. Printed money, the currency of advanced industrial economies, is usually nothing more than a promise by a country's central bank, written on pretty paper. In the United States, the Federal Reserve promise used to include the option to exchange the dollar for gold. Since 1973, this is no longer the case. Now most major currencies are only worth what other people in the market are willing to pay for them. International foreign exchange markets are ruthless in devaluing a currency if it looks as if inflation will make it worth less in the years to come.

Current account. A country's current account measures its international trade during a given period of time. The current account measures "visible" trade, such as imports of videocassette record-ers, and "invisible" trade, which includes services and other pay-ments such as dividends earned from investments abroad. The current account also includes private transfers, such as money sent home by someone working abroad, and official transfers, such as payments to international organizations and interest payments on a country's foreign debt.

Datsu-sara. The Japanese had to invent a word to describe Japanese managers who adopted the Western practice of leaving a company to go their own way. The feudal practice of loyalty to one's over-lord continues in many ways within Japan's modern economy, where workers are expected to remain faithful to one single em-ployer, and vice versa. *Datsu-sara* literally means "corporate drop-out."

Debenture. A debenture is any bond that is backed by nothing more than the good credit of the corporation issuing it. It is an IOU that can be negotiated, bought, or sold by a wide variety of investors. The purchaser of a debenture relies on the "full faith and credit" of the issuer to be paid back. Some debentures are paid off only after other, more senior, creditors have already been paid. These "subordinated" debentures usually provide a higher interest rate to reward the holder for the higher risk.

Debt ratio, debt/equity ratio. A company's health is best determined by comparing how much it owes to how much it owns, or by comparing how much it owes to the equity that stockholders have invested. The basic idea for all of the different debt ratios is the same: if the ratio is high, the company may have borrowed too much and will have trouble paying the interest when it comes due. A company can improve its debt ratios by paying back loans, or by increasing its equity, which means getting stockholders to in-vest more money.

Default. When a country, or a company, is not able to pay its creditors on time, it is said to be in default. The interest payments on notes and bonds are usually the first to be ignored by a debtor in default. If no solution is found, the borrower may even refuse to pay back the principal, the original money borrowed, on its loans. A country in default risks losing all future access to the world economy for trade or further loans.

Deficit. Almost too good to be true, a deficit allows a government or a country to spend what it does not earn. In international economics, there are two major deficits: budget deficits and trade deficits. A government budget deficit occurs when tax revenues are not enough to pay for government spending. To cover a budget deficit, a government usually prints bonds and sells them to the public to make up the difference. A trade deficit is based on the same principle: a country runs a trade deficit when spending on imports exceeds income from exports.

Deflation. Deflation is an economic slowdown. If a country's inflation rate or trade deficits are too high, the government can cool down the economy by raising taxes and reducing spending. During deflation there is less pressure to spend, so prices stop rising and imports are reduced. Deflation can also bring disinflation, a decline in prices, which is the opposite of inflation.

Demand. The part of economics relating to consumption is called demand. It tells us what consumers or businesses will buy at a given price. Economists love drawing graphs called supply and demand curves to explain the very simple idea that when prices change, consumers and producers change their behavior. The basic idea of supply and demand is the following: when prices go up, more goods and services are supplied, but there is less demand from consumers. When prices go down, demand goes up but the supply is reduced. At a certain price level there will be an equilibrium of supply and demand. This pattern can be applied to almost all goods and services.

Depreciation. The reduction of an asset's value over time is called depreciation. Tax authorities allow a company to reduce the value on their books of buildings and other capital goods such as machinery, pickups, and copy machines. A company treats these reductions in value as costs, which allows it to reduce reported earnings. Companies prefer to depreciate as much as they can as early as they can in order to reduce taxes.

Depression. A prolonged economic slowdown is called a depression. It is marked by a decline in production and demand. As a result, companies go bankrupt and unemployment rises. Caused in part by a worldwide trade war, the great international depression of the 1930s made it clear how interconnected the world economy had become. Governments can usually avoid depressions by providing the necessary stimulus, such as an increase in the money supply or an increase in government spending.

Deregulation. "Que será, será—whatever will be will be." Deregulation is the removal of restrictions on companies and agencies in an attempt to encourage competition and make the economy more productive. Under deregulation, industries such as airlines, trucking, or telephone services are allowed to make their own decisions on prices and markets, regardless of the effect on consumers.

Devaluation. When a currency's value is fixed by the government, there comes a time when it is no longer possible to keep it trading at high levels. When speculators start selling the currency on the open markets, the government has to step in and buy large quantities in order to keep its price up. When the government gives up supporting the currency and admits that it should have a lower value, it announces a devaluation. In a system of floating exchange rates, this would not have to happen: a weak currency would depreciate in value gradually.

Diminishing returns. The first part in the process of producing or consuming something is almost always more rewarding than the end. A hungry consumer, for example, will be less willing to pay as much for a second or third piece of expensive cheesecake. In a factory, new machinery is also subject to the laws of diminishing returns. When the first machines are installed, productivity increases quickly. When further machines are installed, productivity still increases, but not as quickly. The return on each new investment is said to be diminishing.

Discount rate. The interest rate that central banks charge for loans to banks and other financial institutions is called the discount rate. It is usually regarded as a benchmark because its movement gives an accurate indication of the direction of the credit market as a whole. In the United States, the discount rate is what the Federal Reserve charges banks that borrow from it. This is not to be confused with "Fed funds," which is the rate banks in the United States charge each other for overnight loans.

Dividend. A cash payment to a company's shareholders is called a dividend. When a company makes a profit, it can be paid directly to the shareholders, or it can be reinvested into the company. In both cases, the shareholder benefits. What is not paid as a dividend increases the value of the company, and the share price usually rises accordingly. Dividends can also be in the form of stock or other securities.

Division of labor. "The butcher, the baker, and the candlestick maker." All modern countries are based on the principle of division of labor. Since no one person is able to effectively produce everything that is needed, work is divided among workers of different skills. A division of labor ensures that each job gets done more efficiently.

Dow Jones industrial average. The Dow Jones industrial average is a summary of the stock prices of thirty of America's premier companies. This average is the most watched indicator of the direction of the U.S. stock market. The thirty blue-chip companies used in the "Dow" include IBM, AT&T, and General Motors.

Dumping. The sale of goods at a price below cost is called dumping. This dubious business practice is used by powerful manufacturers to capture a market. The goal is to drive all competitors out of business and then increase prices at will.

Earnings. A company's earnings is its profits. It is what remains after all the expenses have been deducted from revenue. Earnings, the proverbial bottom line, is also called net income. For an individual, earnings is the total take-home pay, including overtime and bonuses.

Econometrics. Econometrics is the scientific use of statistics and formulas to develop economic theories. Econometricians use complex mathematical models to simulate real-life situations and test the effect on an economy of changes in such factors as interest rates, taxes, and investment.

Economies of scale. "Many hands make light work." Economies of scale are the advantages that come from making many of the same thing at one time. The first automobile assembly lines of the Ford Motor Company used this idea of mass production to produce large quantities of Model-T's at an affordable price. Increased production allows the initial costs of investment to be quickly recovered and each unit is produced more efficiently.

ECU, European currency unit. The ECU was invented by the European Community to provide a single unit of value to facilitate EC accounts. The value of the ECU is determined by the values of all the different EC currencies from the Belgian franc to the Spanish peseta.

Elasticity. Elasticity is the measure of how much something will change, or stretch, given a certain situation. The price elasticity of demand, for example, tells us how much the demand for a product will change given a change in its price. A shopper with high elasticity of demand, for example, will rush out and buy a product if it is on sale. Elasticity can be applied to many economic factors such as supply and demand.

Equilibrium. Classical economics is based on the theory that all forces in an economy will move toward an equilibrium. When the price of a product is neither too high nor too low, there will be an equilibrium where supply equals demand. Alternatively, when wages, the price of labor, are at the right level, inflation and unemployment are said to be in equilibrium. Equilibriums also exist for savings, investment, and other economic factors.

Equity. Equity is ownership. A stockholder has equity in a company just as a homeowner has equity in a house and its property. On a company's balance sheet, the equity section describes the share of a company that belongs to the shareholders, after liabilities have been deducted from assets. A company's net worth, its assets minus liabilities, is called stockholders' equity.

Eurodollar. A "currency abroad," Eurodollars are dollars held in bank accounts anywhere outside of the United States. The term was invented in the 1950s when big holders of dollars, the Soviet Union especially, opened bank accounts in London to keep their holdings away from the control of U.S. authorities. The prefix "Euro" can apply to any currency held outside of its country of origin. A Eurocurrency does not necessarily have to be held on deposit in Europe. French francs held in an account in Canada are called Eurofrancs and Japanese yen held in an account in Hong Kong are called Euroyen.

Euromarkets. Euromarkets refer to the restriction-free markets for stocks, bonds, and other financial instruments that boomed in the 1970s and 1980s, principally in London. The Eurobond market, for example, provided an enormous capital market for all of the Eurodollars and other currencies in offshore accounts. The Euromarkets soon became more popular than domestic markets because of the freedom from local restrictions. Even American corporations found that they could borrow in the Eurobond market more cheaply than in the United States.

Exchange rates. The value of currencies worldwide is provided by exchange rates. A currency, like any other commodity, is worth only what people will pay for it. Exchange rates tell us how many French francs a U.S. dollar is worth, or how many U.S. dollars a British pound is worth.

Federal Reserve. The Federal Reserve fills the role of a central bank for the United States: it manages the money supply, it regulates the banking system, and it acts as a lender of last resort. It answers to no one, except for yearly reports to Congress, so it can act independently. The seven members of the Federal Reserve Board are appointed by the president.

Fiscal policy. Fiscal policy refers to a government's use of taxing and spending powers to influence the economy. A government can give the economy a boost by increasing spending, for example, thereby creating jobs and increasing production.

Flight capital. Flight capital denotes funds transferred abroad by citizens fearful that their own country's economy or laws may make their hard-earned capital worthless in the years ahead. Latin Americans, fearing high inflation in their own countries, buy dollars and send them to accounts in Europe and North America, often in defiance of exchange control laws. Often, the more a country tries to keep money from being sent abroad, the more it encourages flight capital.

Floating rate note (FRN). A floating rate note is a debt security that has its interest rate refixed periodically. Most floating rate notes use LIBOR, the London Interbank Offered Rate, as a reference for determining the interest rate to be paid to the holder. Many banks and investors prefer the price stability of floating rate notes, because during periods of fluctuating interest rates, when fixed-rate bond prices can change dramatically, the prices of FRNs remain relatively stable. In order to remain in line with prevailing interest rates, floating rate notes change their interest payment, not their price.

Foreign exchange. Foreign exchange denotes the market for the many different currencies in the world economy. These currencies trade against each other, as does any other commodity, and their prices are quoted in terms of other currencies. A Swiss franc, for example, is worth a certain amount of Japanese yen. And a New Zealand dollar is worth a certain amount of German marks. Foreign exchange trading takes place twenty-four hours a day, usually on bank trading floors that are connected electronically with other banks all over the world.

Forward markets. Forward markets have been set up to allow for purchases of commodities or financial instruments at a future date. A wheat farmer, for example, could make a forward contract to sell the next year's harvest at today's price. The buyer and the seller both get the security of having the price fixed ahead of the actual delivery. Unlike futures contracts, which are traded on exchanges with fixed prices and dates, forward contracts can be tailor-made to accommodate the needs of different counterparties such as corporate clients or financial institutions. Forward markets exist for a wide range of commodities, currencies, securities, and other financial instruments.

Free-market economy. A free-market economy, where the decisions are left up to the market, is supposed to force producers to offer the right goods at the right prices to consumers. This is the opposite of a centrally planned economy in which the major economic decisions regarding prices and production are fixed by the state.

Friedman, Milton. "Let the markets decide." With followers all over the world, University of Chicago economist Milton Friedman has done more than anyone to promote the ideas of free markets. For decades, "Uncle Miltie" has been calling for a worldwide expansion of free trade and capitalism. "The freedom to choose" is the goal of Friedman economics: if consumers are allowed to buy what they want and producers are free to sell where they want, the world will be made a better place for almost everyone.

Futures. Futures are contracts to buy or sell commodities or financial instruments at a fixed price for a fixed time in the future. Because the time and date conform to other contracts, futures can be traded on exchanges. Financial futures were introduced in Chicago in the 1970s when brokers realized that money and securities, just like other commodities, could be bought and sold for future delivery.

G-7. The "club" of the richest industrial nations, G-7 is the group of the seven largest free-market economies. They meet periodically to discuss common goals and problems and to coordinate economic policy. This select group is made up of the United States, Japan, Germany, France, Britain, Italy, and Canada. The leaders of these "rich" countries usually meet in well-photographed conferences in resorts or capitals of member countries. The European Community as a whole is also represented through an additional delegate.

Game theory. Game theory is a not-so-playful, high-tech way of looking at problems in which all conflicts, including war and trade, can be put into a formula. The most notorious game theory looks at wars as a "zero-sum" game where one side's loss is always the other side's gain: the sum of all the wins and losses is said to equal zero. Trade wars, however, can be worse than a zero-sum game because summing up all the wins and losses can be less than zero where everybody ends up losing. When one side loses the opportunity to sell a useful product on the world markets, it also means a loss for the consumers in the opposing country.

GATT. On the shores of Lake Geneva in Switzerland, the world's major trading nations have formed an organization called GATT, the General Agreement on Tariffs and Trade. It is not just an agreement: it is an organization that monitors and directs trade among its member countries. The goal of GATT is to remove barriers to world trade in goods, services, and ideas. Individual countries with trade disputes can use GATT to negotiate a settlement, avoiding trade wars where everyone gets hurt, not least of all the lowly consumer.

GDP, GNP. The gross domestic product and gross national product measure the total amount of activity in a country's economy. The GDP measures all of a country's domestic production of goods and services. The GNP is a wider measure that includes a country's activities abroad such as exports and imports and income from foreign operations. Neither the GDP nor the GNP tells the whole story, however, because an economy has many unreported activities such as voluntary work, unpaid housework, environmental destruction, and illegal drug trade. Although the GDP and GNP provide only an estimate of the size of an economy, they are the most accurate measures available.

Gearing. Getting more bang for your buck, gearing refers to the amount of debt a company has in relation to its share capital. This is usually called the debt ratio. Just as a bicycle uses a bigger gear on the front sprocket to make the rear wheel go faster, a company can increase its debt to make the stockholders' funds go further. But this debt is not free, and a company may get into trouble if high interest payments cannot be paid on time. For most companies, markets look for a gearing of 1 to 1, where debt is no greater than the stockholders' equity. Gearing of 2 to 1, twice as much debt as equity, is sometimes allowed in certain industries. Gearing also varies from country to country.

Glass-Steagall. In Japan, Britain, and the United States, commercial banks are not allowed to issue and trade securities, and investment banks are not allowed to take deposits and make loans. This separation of investment banking and commercial banking activities dates from the 1930s in the United States where the Glass-

Steagall Act was passed to protect small bank deposits from being lost in risky securities trading. In Japan, the separation was made law by Article 65. Most European countries, with the exception of Britain, do not see a problem in having a bank undertake both investment and commercial banking activities. French, German, and Swiss "universal banks" can do it all.

Golden parachute. Fearing a hostile takeover of their company, the managers of a company will sometimes incorporate huge guaranteed salaries and bonuses into their own pay packages if they are ever forced out. These golden parachutes are supposed to allow them to land on their feet with their pockets full of money if they find themselves out of a job. This comforts management, but it is the stockholders who end up footing the bill.

Greenmail. In a takeover or a leveraged buyout, it is sometimes easier to get opponents to change their course of action by offering them a big financial reward. Greenmail refers to the use of financial incentives, such as buying back their shares at lucrative prices, to get them to abandon a hostile takeover attempt.

Hedge. A hedge, as the name implies, provides a barrier, a protection from uncertainty. A hedge is buying or selling something to protect an investment from unwelcome change in the market. An owner of stocks who thinks the market will go down can hedge by buying put options that give the right to sell at a high price if the market drops. Many investors hedge against inflation by buying real assets like real estate or gold.

High net worth individual. The kind of client most banks dream about, a high net worth individual has a lot of disposable assets and few liabilities. Banks around the world have discovered the advantages of having high net worth individuals as clients and are building up private banking operations in all of the major financial capitals. In New York, London, Paris, Geneva, Zurich, Tokyo, and Hong Kong, banks have set up facilities to cater to the needs of these big spenders.

Hot money. Money invested in banks for very short periods, such as overnight deposits, is called hot money. This money comes into banks around the world as short-term investments, in search of the highest return. It can also leave at a moment's notice, which worries central bankers and finance ministers, who fear the day when the hot money is withdrawn to chase a higher real interest rate somewhere else in the world.

Hyperinflation. Hyperinflation is prices rising out of control, sometimes exceeding 1,000 percent per year. It usually occurs in countries with severe economic problems, such as Germany in the 1920s and Latin America in the 1980s.

Import substitution. Import substitution is a government policy that forces consumers to replace imports with locally produced goods and services. This policy was widely implemented in indebted Latin American countries in the 1980s. The goal is to save precious foreign reserves. The problem is that most countries cannot produce efficiently without the help of imported computers or tractors, and the whole economy suffers for lack of productive tools. Free trade always suffers when barriers such as import substitution force countries to buy only local products, because those countries needing to export the most usually end up producing noncompetitive products for the world markets.

Incomes policy. An inflation-control plan that reduces consumers' real disposable income is called incomes policy. It is often used in Third World countries to control rampaging inflation by reducing consumer spending. In order to stabilize prices, incomes policy uses measures such as wage freezes to stabilize consumers' disposable income.

Inflation. Inflation is the percentage increase in prices in an economy, usually measured by an index of consumer prices such as the consumer price index (CPI). Many central bankers see inflation as the world's greatest economic evil and make it their policy to control it at all costs, even if it means bringing on an economic recession. Inflation is seen as hurting almost everyone in an economy, including consumers, producers, and old-age pensioners.

Insider trading. A company's insiders are those who have advance knowledge of financial statements and other company secrets. They can benefit from inside information to trade the company's stocks and options. In some countries, such as Hong Kong,

France, and Switzerland, insider trading was not traditionally considered a crime. Insiders were seen as just the first in line for getting the news about a company. This "first come, first served" mentality usually means that insiders start trading before the small investor has a chance. Because of intense international pressure, insider trading has now been made illegal in almost every major market in the world.

Institutional investors. Institutions, such as insurance companies and pension funds, have trillions of dollars, yen, marks, and pounds to invest in the world markets at any given time. Their decisions dwarf most other players in the international markets, including many governments. The biggest institutional investors in the world often come from Japan, where the high savings rate has created a mountain of money that needs to be invested in markets around the world.

Interbank market. The interest rates that banks charge for loans to other banks are usually the lowest in the market. Interbank rates are often used as a benchmark for other lending. For example, the London Interbank Offered Rate (LIBOR) is used around the world as a base for fixing the interest rate on many loans and securities.

International Development Association (IDA). The IDA is an arm of the World Bank that lends to the world's poorest countries at generous conditions, such as a zero rate of interest and lengthy repayment time. Many IDA loans are not expected to be repaid. The loans are financed by contributions from the governments of wealthy nations.

International Finance Corporation (IFC). The IFC is the arm of the World Bank that makes loans and takes equity stakes in private companies in the developing countries.

International Monetary Fund (IMF). The problems of the world's debtor countries are so complex that the World Bank and other international lenders will agree to new loans only if the country agrees to an economic austerity plan, usually prescribed by the IMF. The International Monetary Fund was established at the same time as the World Bank to regulate the world's exchange rates, but has now assumed a leading role in restructuring debtor countries' economies and providing short-term loans.

Investment. Economists use this word to define a specific economic activity: the purchase of productive assets, such as factories, equipment, houses, and vehicles. In this sense, investment can be used to power economic growth.

Investment bank. "Masters of the financial universe," investment banks in the United States and Japan underwrite new issues of securities such as stocks and bonds and trade these securities for their clients and for their own accounts. This was considered a risky undertaking in the 1930s, so the United States passed a law to separate investment banks from commercial banks, which take deposits and make loans. In England, investment banks are called merchant banks. In the rest of Europe, "universal banks" are allowed to act as both investment banks and commercial banks. Investment banks are also called securities houses.

Invisible hand. The idea of the invisible hand was formulated by Adam Smith in the eighteenth century to explain how the markets, if left to themselves, will find the most efficient path. The invisible hand of the marketplace refers to the result of millions of profit-seeking consumers and producers making rational decisions. They are expected to make the right decisions without the state or anyone else telling them how.

Invisible trade. Invisible trade consists of exports and imports of services such as banking and insurance and other nontangible trade such as films and television programs. It also includes interest and dividend payments from foreign investments. One of the most important invisible trades is tourism: some countries, Germany and Japan for example, have invisible trade deficits because of all the money their citizens spend abroad while traveling.

Joint venture. A joint venture involves two or more companies, joining together, usually to own another company. In order to compete in difficult foreign markets, many companies prefer joint ventures with a local partner to take advantage of their knowledge and skills in the domestic market.

Junk bonds. Companies with low credit ratings often have to issue bonds with high interest rates in order to get needed capital for expansion or takeovers. These lower-than-investment-grade bonds are often called junk bonds. The investment banks that issue them prefer to call them high-yield securities.

Keiretsu. *Keiretsu* is the Japanese word describing the tightly organized system of interlocking corporations with multiple layers of middlemen and brand-loyal retailers that effectively allows Japan to limit imports of foreign products.

Keynesian economics. John Maynard Keynes, a British economist, was one of the most influential figures in the world during the Great Depression. His ideas on using government spending to combat economic recession contributed to one of the most important advances in modern economics. Keynesian economics relies on the use of government spending to control the economy, calling for overspending with deficits during times of economic depression and underspending with surpluses during times of too-rapid economic growth. Most politicians are easily convinced to use deficit spending to stimulate the economy, but are decidedly un-Keynesian when it comes to spending less during periods of rapid economic growth.

Laffer curve. The Laffer curve relates the reduction of taxes to an increase in economic activity. The idea is simple, and it had many fans in the United States during the early years of the Reagan presidency. The government was supposed to lower taxes, and get government off people's backs. The tax breaks were then supposed to increase economic activity, which would bring in more taxes. The Reagan administration, however, somehow ended up doubling the national debt, something that most supply-siders did not find amusing.

Laissez faire. Laissez faire is a French term meaning "let them do it." It is used to describe the government policy that lets the markets decide what is best. Consumers and producers are expected to come to the right decisions on their own.

Leading economic indicators. The statistics prepared by governments to plot the course of future economic activity are called leading economic indicators. They track such things as retail sales, industrial output, housing starts, and financial activity. Economic statistics that show where the economy has been, such as unemployment figures, are called lagging economic indicators.

Letter of credit. In international trade, a letter of credit is used by an importer to provide a guarantee that funds are available to pay for the goods sent from abroad. A foreign supplier will ship the goods only when a reputable bank has provided the necessary letter of credit.

Leveraged buyout. A leveraged buyout is the use of borrowed money to take over a company. The buyer puts up a small amount of capital and uses huge amounts of debt to buy a company, often over the protests of the company's management. The leveraged buyouts that fueled the takeover craze of the 1980s were supposed to make everyone happy: the bondholders, the stockholders, the new owners, and the investment banks who got big fees for their advice and for issuing the junk bonds sometimes used to pay for the buyout. The only problem is that with so much debt, highly leveraged companies have to struggle to meet the enormous interest payments, and sometimes they go bankrupt.

Liabilities. A liability is a debt or other anticipated obligation. On a balance sheet, liabilities are on the right side. They balance the assets listed on the left side. Stockholders' equity is the amount by which assets exceed liabilities. Current liabilities are those that have to be paid off in twelve months or less. Any longer liability is called long-term debt.

Liquidity. Liquidity means a ready supply of funds. In a nation's money supply, liquidity refers to the funds that are injected and drained by the central bank. In a company's balance sheet, liquidity is a measure of the company's ability to come up with the cash to pay its debts. In the securities market, a bond is said to be liquid if it can be easily traded in large size with no effect on the price.

Lombard Rate. The interest rate that Germany's Bundesbank and other central banks charge on collateralized loans to banks is called the Lombard Rate. The banks borrowing the money usually put up government bonds as collateral in order to receive the preferential Lombard Rates. The name is based on Europe's early bankers, who, more often than not, came from Lombardia, the northern Italian region around Milan.

Macroeconomics. Macroeconomics, the "big picture," is the study of an economy's aggregate factors such as growth, unemployment, inflation, and government spending. The other side of the economy, the "small picture" of individuals and firms, is called microeconomics.

Margin. Most brokers allow clients to open a margin account to purchase more securities than their cash will allow. The broker lends the investor money to buy stocks and other financial instruments that are used as collateral for the loans. The investor pays interest on this borrowed money. If the value of the securities drops below a certain level, the investor will be asked to put in more money or sell the securities. This moment of truth is referred to as a margin call.

Marginal analysis. The study of behavior at the edges, or how people or firms behave when given the option of having "one more" of something is called marginal analysis. The additional "one thin wafer," for example, is not as appetizing after having just consumed a huge meal. There is a diminishing return as more is consumed or saved or spent or earned. Marginal propensity to consume, like other marginal propensities, refers to how much the next good or action is worth. And then the next one after that.

Market-maker. "Bid, 25—offer, 26. What do you wanna do? You wanna buy or you wanna sell?" A market-maker will make a two-way price for almost anything. For most securities—such as stocks and bonds—the price at which the market-maker buys is called a bid. It is always lower than the price at which the market-maker will sell, called an offer, or "asked" price in the United States. The market-maker makes money on the spread, the difference between the bid and offer.

Marx, Karl. "The father of communism." The German economic philosopher and sociologist Karl Marx wrote the first major work on communism, *Das Kapital.* In it he foresaw the demise of capitalism and the creation of a socialist economic system based on the philosophy of "from each according to his abilities, to each according to his needs." Marx's pessimistic view of capitalism was based on the terrible inequities he saw in England in the nineteenth century. He called for a "dictatorship of the proletariat," where the workers would replace the capitalist ruling class. Ironically, his "communist" revolution did not occur in the industrialized West as he expected, but in rural Russia where it eventually was deformed by the excesses of the Stalin regime.

Mean, median. The terms *mean* and *median* are often confused. The simple average is called the mean. It is calculated by adding up a list and then dividing by the number of items in the list to give the average. The mean is used for calculating most things, such as average income. Sometimes, however, it is useful to do a more complicated analysis and look at the way figures are distributed. In a series of numbers, for example, the median is the point at which 50 percent of the numbers are higher and 50 percent are lower.

Mercantilism. Mercantilism is the policy of using balance of trade surpluses to accumulate wealth and power. It emphasizes exports over imports. A mercantilist economy aims to produce goods for export instead of for domestic consumption. A mercantilist country, such as Japan in the 1980s, ends up with fewer goods for its consumers but with a high level of savings and international investment.

Merchant banking. In the United States, the term *merchant banking* is used to describe the practice of investment banks investing their own money in their clients' projects. Securities houses are called investment banks in the U.S. and merchant banks in the U.K.

Mergers and acquisitions. Mergers and acquisitions designates the activities where companies are bought, sold, or joined together. During the 1980s, creative financing allowed companies and investors to go on a shopping spree, buying undervalued companies, merging parts of them with existing operations, and selling off other parts to other investors playing the M&A game.

Microeconomics. The study of the activities of an economy's individuals and firms is called microeconomics. It is the opposite of macroeconomics, which looks at the big picture. Microeconomics, like a microscope, looks at the smaller things, such as the behavior of individuals and how firms make their decisions under various economic conditions.

Monetarism. The economic theory that is based on the belief that changes in the money supply can be used to control economic growth is called monetarism. Monetarists believe that inflation, for example, can best be controlled by reducing the money supply. When the economy appears to be overheating, the central bank can simply reduce the money supply, which increases interest rates and slows down the economy.

Money market. The money market consists of all the world's short-term investments of money. This includes overnight deposits such as interbank deposits, Treasury bills, or fiduciary deposits. In these short-term borrowing and lending operations, money is bought and sold at a price, its interest rate. The price of money, like that of all other scarce commodities, is determined by supply and demand.

Money supply. A country's money supply has many different components, ranging from coins and notes to deposits in savings accounts. The money supply most talked about is the M1, which consists of all notes and coins in circulation and money in bank accounts, such as checking accounts, which can be withdrawn at a moment's notice. Other broader measures of the money supply, such as M3 and M4, include money in less easily available deposits, such as time-deposits and other long-term investments.

Monopoly. A monopoly is complete control of one sector of production within an economy. The sole producer of a good can exploit a monopoly to raise prices without limit. There are very few real monopolies. Consumers usually find an alternative. The OPEC oil producers thought they had a near monopoly in the 1970s when they dramatically raised oil prices, but consumers found alternative sources of fuel. Antitrust laws are used to restrict monopolies in most countries.

Moody's, Standard & Poor's. The two largest credit ratings services in the world, Moody's Investors Services and Standard & Poor's, are both based in New York. They provide an up-to-date analysis of the financial health of companies, countries, and other borrowers around the world. Their stamp of top quality, the "AAA," is awarded only to the world's most credit-worthy borrowers, such as Japan, the United States, the World Bank, IBM, and Sweden.

Multilateral trade agreements. When several trading partners agree on a common trade policy, usually under the guidance of the General Agreement on Tariffs and Trade (GATT), it means that the consumers may choose the best from around the world, at the best prices. The goal of most multilateral trade agreements is to remove barriers to trade. The European Common Market is one of the world's most successful examples of a multilateral trade agreement.

Multinationals. A company with operations in different countries is called a multinational. Once scorned by the world as symbols of capitalist imperialism, multinational companies are now courted by most countries to bring needed capital and jobs. The elimination of trade barriers, in the European Common Market for example, has made it possible for a company to market a product in several countries at the same time. Multinationals take advantage of the global marketplace to produce and sell in many countries at once.

Mutual fund. A mutual fund is a collection of bonds or stocks that allows investors to avoid risking all their money on one single company. Each share in a mutual fund represents a part of a well-diversified portfolio. Mutual funds are especially appropriate for international investments where information on foreign companies and markets is not accessible to the individual investor.

Net assets. What a company really "owns," net assets is what is left when a company's liabilities are subtracted from its assets. Stockholders regard net assets as their share of the company, also called shareholders' equity.

Newly Industrialized Countries (NIC). The Newly Industrialized Countries are those lucky Third World countries that are well on their way to joining the ranks of the developed countries. Most lists of NICs include Brazil, Israel, Hong Kong, the Philippines, Singapore, South Africa, South Korea, Taiwan, Thailand, and Yugoslavia.

Offshore banking. Offshore banking refers to all those banking activities that are free of domestic restrictions and regulations. In order to compete with traditional offshore banking centers like the Bahamas, traditional banking centers like New York have set up facilities to cater to the needs of clients looking to put their money in tax-free accounts. Other offshore banking centers include London, Luxembourg, Singapore, and Hong Kong.

Open market operations. Central banks use open market operations to buy and sell securities. This has the effect of controlling the money supply because money held at central banks, such as the U.S. Federal Reserve, is not considered part of the money supply, and when it is used to buy securities on the open market, the money supply is increased. Alternatively, when central banks sell securities on the open market, the money supply is reduced by the amount paid into the central banks' vaults. The securities bought and sold by central banks in open market operations are usually government bonds.

Organization of Petroleum Exporting Countries (OPEC). The oil producers' "club," OPEC was established in 1960 to coordinate the policies of a large part of the world's oil producers. The oil shocks of the 1970s were a result of OPEC's decision to restrict production and drive up prices. The members of OPEC are Saudi Arabia, Iran, Iraq, Kuwait, the United Arab Emirates, Qatar, Venezuela, Nigeria, Libya, Indonesia, Algeria, Gabon, and Ecuador.

Over-the-counter (OTC). Over-the-counter shares usually trade electronically, not on the major stock exchanges. OTC stocks are almost always for smaller companies that do not meet the strict financial requirements to trade on established exchanges. OTC stocks trade on electronic exchanges such as NASDAQ in the United States, the USM (Unlisted Securities Market) in Britain, and the OTC and Tokyo "second section" stock exchanges in Japan.

Par. When a bond or a fixed-income stock is worth 100 percent of its nominal value, it is said to trade at par. For most bonds, par is $1,000, and for most fixed-income stocks, par is $100. The price of most bonds or shares does not stay at par. When interest rates rise or fall, for example, the price of a bond that was trading at 100 percent of its nominal value has to rise above par or drop below par to make the bond's return competitive with other bonds in the market.

Per capita. Latin for "per head," per capita can also be translated as "per person." A very useful concept in comparing countries, it puts all total figures on a human scale. For example, it was misleading to call Brazil the world's biggest Third World debtor in the 1980s, because the debt was applied to a country with a population of 120 million people. Argentina had a smaller total debt, but its debt per capita was much higher than Brazil's because its total debt was applied to a country with a much smaller population.

Per capita GNP. One of the best ways to measure a country's wealth is to look at its per capita GNP. It measures the total output of goods and services of a country that can be applied to each person in the country. At 1988 levels, for example, the per capita GNP of Japan was $23,300, while that for the United States was $18,500. Even though the United States produced more total goods and services, the per capita GNP in Japan was higher.

Perestroika. Russian for "economic restructuring." When it became apparent in the 1980s that the Soviet Union's economy was becoming strangled by bureaucracy, party leader Mikhail Gorbachev called for a system of economic reforms called perestroika. The goal was to make the economy more efficient by decentralizing decision making. The country was then supposed to move toward a system where the market would decide how much would be produced and how the resources would be distributed.

Poison pill. When a company wants to defend itself against a hostile takeover, it can undertake to render the company unattractive through a series of financial maneuvers called a poison pill defense. A drastic increase in debt, for example, makes the company less attractive financially. A poison pill defense often succeeds in keeping the company in the hands of the original owners, but they may find that it has irreparably harmed the company itself.

Preferred stock. Preferred stock is equity that pays a dividend at a fixed rate. In many ways, it is more like a bond in that its fixed dividend resembles an interest payment. Preferred stock, as the name implies, is considered to be senior to common stock except it does not ordinarily carry voting rights. If a company goes bankrupt, holders of preferred stock are paid off before those holding common stock.

Primary market. When bonds and stocks are issued, they are traded in a "primary" market until they are ready to be treated like all the other "seasoned" securities. A primary market for bonds will usually exist until the payment date, when the bond starts paying interest. Then it trades in the secondary market. Primary market trading normally takes place outside of established trading exchanges.

Prime rate. The prime rate is the interest rate banks charge their best corporate customers. This follows the traditional guideline for bank lending: "low risk, low reward." The bank's other, more risky, customers are lent money at a higher rate, which is based on the prime rate. When the prime rate goes down, most other rates are lowered as well.

Principal. Principal is the face value of a loan. When the borrower pays back the principal, the loan is paid off. Until the principal is paid off, most borrowers make periodic interest payments that are based, as a percentage, on the outstanding principal. The principal on some loans, such as those to Third World countries, may never be paid back at all. In the meantime, the creditors just try to collect as much interest as they can.

Private placement. A private placement is an issue of equity or debt securities that is too small to treat as a public placement. There are less reporting requirements on private placements, and the bonds, or notes, are sometimes not traded on the open market. The securities issued in a private placement are often sold to a small group of institutional investors.

Privatization. A government's "going out of business" sale, privatiza-

tion is the sale of government-owned companies. Usually inefficient and a drain on government resources, government companies such as steel mills are often the result of previous
nationalizations. When the government decides that its companies can be run more efficiently in the private sector, it sells its
share in the company to private investors.

Productivity. "Output per capita," productivity compares the amount
of goods or services produced to the amount of people, capital, or
land used in the production process. When machines are used to
do the jobs people once performed, labor productivity usually
increases. In another case, when people work more efficiently,
labor productivity goes up because more goods are produced by
the same amount of people.

Purchasing power parity (PPP). The cost of an average "basket" of
goods and services in each country can serve as a basis for comparing the value of different countries' currencies. Since exchange
rates are determined by the foreign exchange markets and not by
what the currency can really buy in its home market, it is often
useful to look at a currency's purchasing power, called purchasing
power parity (PPP), to compare figures in different currencies. For
example, the yen's value on the foreign exchange market tells us
how many yen can be bought for a hundred U.S. dollars, but it
does not tell us what a hundred dollars' worth of yen will really
buy in Tokyo. PPP provides an alternative to exchange rates to
translate values from one currency into another.

Quota. A quota is a limit on the quantity of a good that may be
imported over a certain period of time. A government unwilling
to open its borders to free trade will set a quota on imported goods
to protect local producers who are not efficient enough to compete
on world markets. The result is often a decline in the standard
of living as quality foreign goods are kept from the domestic consumers.

Rational expectations. Much of modern economics is based on the
theory of rational expectations, the belief that people, when armed
with all the available information, will act logically. Unfortunately,
many consumers and producers do not always act rationally, and

economic theories based on the theory of rational expectations will often be flawed.

Reaganomics. Once called "voodoo economics" by rival candidate George Bush, Ronald Reagan's plan for the American economy in the 1980s advocated reducing taxes to increase economic growth. According to Reaganomics, the tax cuts would lead to reduced government spending and America would be better off. In fact, the Reagan regime reduced social spending but increased government spending for defense, and the United States under Reaganomics doubled its national debt to $3 trillion.

Real values. Values that have been adjusted for inflation are referred to as real values. In inflationary times, prices often go up so quickly it is difficult to compare one nominal value to another. By adjusting all statistics for inflation, it is possible to compare their "real" values.

Receivables. "Counting your chickens before they're hatched." On a balance sheet, something owed to the company is considered to be an asset even before it is actually paid. These assets are called receivables. When receivables are paid, they become current assets.

Recession. A recession is a prolonged economic slowdown. The world has become so interconnected that an economic recession in one country will often spread to the rest. The first signs of a recession are usually a decline in economic indicators such as housing starts and retail sales. When a country enters a full-blown recession, unemployment rises sharply and interest rates usually decline.

Repurchase agreements. The purchase of bonds with the agreement to sell them back at a date sometime in the future is called a repurchase agreement. The terms of the "repo," as it is called in the market, are fixed in advance. Like a short-term deposit, the buyer holds the bonds for only a short period of time. When a central bank like the U.S. Federal Reserve wants interest rates to go down, it buys bonds through repurchase agreements in the open market, which increases the money supply. More money in the market means lower interest rates. When traders see the

"Fed" doing repos, they expect a decline in interest rates, so they rush out to buy bonds.

Rescheduling. When confronted with borrowers who cannot immediately repay their loans, creditor banks sometimes reschedule the loans to give the debtors more time to come up with the money. Rescheduling has become a popular way to deal with problem loans to many Third World countries because it allows both creditors and debtors to avoid admitting that the loans will never be paid off. If the banks do not reschedule, the borrower goes into default, and the loans are written off as a loss on the bank's books.

Savings. Savings is income that is not spent. In the 1980s, while the Italians and the Japanese were saving up to a third of their salaries, the average American was saving only half that much. Because savings usually translates into greater investment in the economy, those countries with high savings rates usually have greater long-term growth.

Savings and Loan (S&L). A financial institution that lends money, usually to purchase real estate, such as homes and office buildings. Deposits are principally from local consumers. S&Ls got into big trouble in the 1980s when they used their guaranteed deposits to build an empire of S&L debt—including many "junk bonds"—to lend to risky real estate ventures.

Securities. Worth more than the paper they are printed on, a security is any financial instrument—usually printed on pieces of paper—that represents something of value. In international finance, examples of securities are stocks, bonds, notes, certificates of deposit, and bills. An IOU, for example, is a security written on a piece of paper that states that the holder of the paper is entitled to something of value, usually money. Securities are valuable as long as the buyer is confident that the security can be redeemed for its stated worth. In the 1980s banks began securitizing most of their assets, which meant turning loans and mortgages into pieces of paper that could be negotiated, bought and sold on the world markets.

Short selling. In most markets, investors are allowed to sell stock or other securities they do not own, as long as they agree to provide the securities at some time in the future. This practice is called short selling. A short seller can usually borrow the shares while waiting to buy them at a later date. An investor who takes the view that a stock's price will go down, for example, will sell short, thinking that the shares can be bought back later after the shares' price has fallen.

Smith, Adam. The father of modern economics, Adam Smith was an enlightened eighteenth-century Scotsman who believed that the markets could take care of themselves. He introduced the world to terms like *invisible hand* and *division of labor,* which he used to describe the workings of the free-market economy. His book, *The Wealth of Nations,* provided the foundation for the capitalist economic system. The host of the eponymous U.S. public television show on economics even went so far as to take the name Adam Smith in homage to this great founder of modern economic theory.

Socialism. The term *socialism* refers to a wide variety of political/economic systems that attempt to provide a more equal distribution of wealth. There are many free-market socialist countries, such as France, Spain, or Sweden. The countries of the Soviet bloc, before they reformed their centrally planned economies, were also called socialist countries. The term socialism is often confusing because it refers both to a form of government and to an economic system. Americans usually equate socialism with communism, which is misleading. Many capitalist free-market countries are led by socialist governments. Paris, for example, did not stop being an elegant, bustling capital just because the French elected a socialist government.

Special Drawing Right (SDR). SDRs were created by the International Monetary Fund to provide an alternative to gold and currencies such as the U.S. dollar and German mark for settling international transactions. Many countries have begun to use SDRs as a reserve currency, gradually replacing the dollar. The assets and liabilities of the World Bank and the IMF are denominated in Special Drawing Rights to avoid the confusion of using any one national currency. SDRs can be bought and sold just like any other currency. Their value is based on a basket of sixteen major currencies, such as the U.S. dollar, the Japanese yen, and the German mark.

Speculation. A speculator deals in the commodity and currency markets for the simple purpose of making money. Three kinds of players participate in the international markets: speculators, hedgers, and arbitragers. Speculators think they know something the rest of the market has not yet figured out, and they act on it.

Spot market. A spot trade is executed for immediate delivery and payment. The alternative to spot trading is to buy or sell in the forward or futures markets where trades are executed at various prices for delivery sometime in the future.

Stagflation. Where stagnation meets inflation, economic stagnation and high inflation can occur simultaneously. This phenomenon rarely occurs, because inflation is usually the product of a booming economy, and when the economy stagnates the inflation rate usually drops. Stagflation, however, is a worst-of-both-worlds scenario. It usually occurs when inflationary pressures are so strong that even an economic downturn is unable to quell the pressure toward rising prices.

Stock. Stock is ownership in a corporation. It is represented by units of ownership called shares. A stockholder, also called a shareholder or shareowner, has a claim to the earnings and assets of a company. The company's management is employed by the stockholders to run the company, and if a profit is made, it is either distributed as a dividend to the stockholders or reinvested in the company, increasing the assets owned by the stockholders. The word *stock* is also used to describe inventories.

Stockholders' equity. Stockholders' equity, also called shareholders' equity, is a company's assets minus its liabilities. If a company were to use its assets to pay off all of its debts, whatever would be left is called stockholders' equity. Stockholders' equity is also called net worth.

Subsidy. A subsidy is a government payment to a business, allowing its products to compete with foreign products. Most subsidies are criticized for rewarding inefficiency. Farm subsidies, for example, often encourage inefficient uses of land and labor. In many countries, state-supported industries such as steel and automobiles depend on generous state subsidies to stay in operation.

Supply side. Supply side economics is based on the view that producers can stimulate economic growth better than governments as long as they are given enough tax breaks and reduced regulations. The idea is that once producers start increasing production, they will hire new employees who will use their new salaries to go out and buy new goods and services. Supply side economics is meant to provide an alternative to "demand side" economic systems where governments pump money into the economy through generous spending programs.

Surplus. A surplus occurs when more of something is coming in than going out. In a trade surplus, for example, the money earned from exports is greater than money spent on imports. A government surplus occurs when tax receipts exceed expenditures.

Synergy. "You scratch my back and I'll scratch yours." Synergy is the combining of skills for mutual gain. In trade, synergy refers to the benefits to the world economy of letting countries export those goods and services that they produce most efficiently. Synergy allows each country to be better off by trading its goods and services around the world.

Takeover. A takeover involves controlling enough shares to take command of a company. In a leveraged buyout, for example, a company with a healthy balance sheet and undervalued assets is targeted by arbitragers with large amounts of borrowed money. After gaining control, the takeover group restructures the company and sells off undervalued assets in order to pay off the debt acquired in the takeover.

Tangible net worth. Being discriminating about assets, tangible net worth is an accounting tool that evaluates a company by looking at only its tangible assets and its liabilities. All of the nontangible assets such as goodwill and brand names are removed from the balance sheet before calculating a company's tangible net worth.

A brand name is an intangible asset, because even though it can be bought and sold, it does not represent any tangible value like office buildings and machinery.

Tariffs. A tariff is a tax on imports. Tariffs are trade barriers that one country uses to make imports from other countries more expensive. Although most governments say their goal is free trade, they often let themselves be convinced by local companies to provide some protection against lower-priced and often higher-quality foreign imports. Tariffs allow domestic producers to sell their products unencumbered by low-cost foreign competition. Unfortunately, it is often the consumers who have to pay the cost of higher prices for the domestic products that are protected by tariffs.

Tax haven. A tax haven is a country, often a small island nation with little local industry, where income and profits are not taxed or are taxed at a very low rate. Many companies prefer to set up in tax havens such as the Bahamas or the Cayman Islands in order to avoid paying taxes on their profits.

Third World. The Third World includes the world's poor and developing countries. Some Third World countries are doing so well that they are almost ready to join the ranks of the developed industrialized countries. These lucky few are called Newly Industrialized Countries, or NICs. The rest are struggling to increase economic production to allow their growing populations to enjoy a minimum of economic prosperity. Those that are so poor that they are not developing at all are sometimes called "Fourth World" countries.

Trade balance, balance of trade. A country's trade balance, or balance of trade, is not really a balance. It is simply a measure of the total exports and imports of merchandise. It does not include the trade in services and investments that make up the country's "wider" measure of trade: the current account.

Unemployment. Unemployment is the percentage of an economy's work force that is out of work. Some unemployment statistics include only those actually looking for work, while others include all those citizens not currently employed. Most economists see some unemployment as a necessary evil, because when a certain part of the population is looking for a job, there is less pressure for wage increases, and inflation is kept under control.

Unilateral trade restrictions. A unilateral trade restriction is the decision by a country to impose trade barriers such as tariffs or quotas without prior agreement with its trading partners. Unilateral trade restrictions are often answered by trade restrictions in other countries and before long, a trade war is under way. Organizations like GATT, the General Agreement on Tariffs and Trade, try to bring together all the trading nations of the world to reach multilateral trade agreements, with the intention of increasing trade and thereby increasing world prosperity.

Value added tax (VAT). A tax applied at each stage of production is called a value added tax. Every time the product's value is increased, a tax on the added value has to be paid. In contrast to a sales tax, which is paid by the consumer at the point of sale, a value added tax is paid by all parties in the production process. VAT is used in almost all modern industrial economies to distribute the tax burden more evenly among both producers and consumers.

Velocity. Economists use the word *velocity* to describe a country's economic activity in relation to its money supply, the "speed of money." When a country is able to produce a high GNP on a small money supply, it is said to have a high velocity of circulation.

Venture capital. Venture capital is money that is invested in companies with a potential for rapid growth. Start-up companies looking to grow quickly usually turn to venture capital funds or other investors to obtain the needed capital for their high-risk ventures.

Volatility. Volatility refers to movement of a price or another measure over a given period of time. It includes both frequency of movement and size. A stock, for example, that moves often and widely in any direction is said to be highly volatile. The volatility of stocks, bonds, commodities, and indexes is one factor in determining their price: stock investors, for example, want to be rewarded for the higher risk resulting from higher volatility.

Wage-price spiral. A wage-price spiral is the rapid growth of inflation resulting from a vicious circle of wage increases followed by price increases followed by wage increases, etc. Like the proverbial chicken and egg, it is difficult to determine which came first, and even more difficult to find a way to break the inflationary wage-price spiral.

Warrant. A warrant gives the holder a certain right, usually to buy a company's stock. Just as a warrant in the Old West gave a bounty hunter the right to arrest a wanted criminal, a gold warrant gives the holder the right to buy a certain amount of gold at a certain price. Many warrants are issued with bonds or common stock and give the holder the right to purchase additional stock at a favorable price. Other warrants are issued and sold separately and can be used to purchase gold, currencies, and shares. Because they are issued in limited amounts, warrants are different from options, which are supplied according to demand.

Withholding tax. A withholding tax is deducted at the time an income is received. In most countries, stock dividends and bond interest payments are subject to a withholding tax that allows the tax authorities to receive their money before it goes into the pocket of the investor.

Yield. "Many happy returns!" Yield is the return on an investment, stated in percentage terms. When a ten-year bond is said to be yielding 8 percent, the purchaser receives a return of 8 percent every year until maturity. In order to compare different investments with different interest rates, prices, and maturities, it is useful to calculate their annual percentage return. Yields can be applied to almost any investment in the world economy.